ecoLife:

Your Guide to Living in harmony with the Planet: Save money, Gain health, and contribute to a Better World for the next Generations.

Black and White Edition

Dr. Sandra. Cruz-Pol, Ph.D.

Title in Spanish
EcoVida: Guía para vivir en armonía con el Planeta: ISBN-13: 9781521325476
Also available in digital Kindle version.

ISBN-13: **9781695334571**

Contact information:
https://sites.google.com/view/sandraxpol

Follow me in Twitter https://twitter.com/SXpol

THANK YOU!

I want to thank all the people who came to my night and day with questions about how to make their daily decisions and modify their habits in a way that would have less impact on the planet we live on. They inspired me to continue researching, examining scientific studies, and learning about ecological measures in harmony with the planet. In the long run we can all gain health, energy, and the satisfaction of knowing that you are doing the right thing.

Since I arrived at the University of Puerto Rico in Mayagüez with a doctorate related to studies of gases in the atmosphere using satellite and ground-based sensors, many people asked me to offer talks about climate change and global warming. I got to use countless weekends and evenings to give talks all over the island. Sometimes to small groups of 10-20 people, others to groups of as many as 500 science and math teachers. There was great interest in learning about the causes and effects of climate change. But there came a time when I got weary of talking only about the problem and decided to focus on the Solutions.

I started buying books and doing research in my spare time about all the possible solutions to this crisis. From the beginning I noticed that the solutions were not unique, nor were them in a single discipline, but they required knowledge from multiple disciplines! So, I started reading books, scientific journals, and other resources in areas as varied as organic agriculture, renewable energy, natural medicine, and many others that kept coming up every time someone came to consult me with their questions about it. After more than 10 years and after many research and consultations with experts in the various areas, I learned a lot and I continue to learn because scientific knowledge keeps evolving, in all science disciplines.

Engineers, farmers, doctors, and regular citizens, continue to use their creativity to invent ingenious and innovative ideas to construct a better world. Learning about all these efforts, many times anonymous, I have come to the certainty that there is great hope for this planet if everyone does their part, including governments, but everything starts with Education. And that is the main reason for this book.

TABLE OF CONTENTS

WHY THIS BOOK

There are many reasons why I decided to write this book, I could mention as many as the trivial ones: climate change, the energy crisis, the fall in the global economy, the global health problems. Anyway, I write it because I think it is necessary ... But most of all my inspiration is the many people who suggested it to me; people who attended my talks or workshops, who had access to the web page that I developed when I founded and directed the Green Campus (CV) initiative of the University of Puerto Rico in Mayagüez (UPRM) since 2007 or people who followed me in some of the social networks like Facebook or Twitter.

Most people felt inundated with so much contradictory information; They did not know what to believe. This is due in part to what is known as 'greenwashing', which is nothing more than marketing campaigns that make people believe that a product is eco-friendly when it is not, including misleading information on labels. In addition, it is due to the propagation of false information from climate denies most of whom have interests in petroleum industries and want to keep human activities business as usual.

Numerous people wrote to me via email. Facebook, and other means, to ask me about which product to buy or which article to believe. I even got inquiries from outside Puerto Rico, including people from Latin American countries and several times from Florida and Texas, two U.S. states where there are many Spanish speakers. This is so because the website was in that language. Later on, after I published the book in Spanish, I was asked by English-speaking friends to please translate to this language.

I understood then that there is still a lack of conclusive information on all these issues that are increasingly important for the health of the planet and to alleviate the greatest crisis that the human race has experienced. I realized that I had a mission and that I had to find time outside of my regular work schedule, sometimes devoting long weekend hours during weeks and months, to write all this science-based knowledge in an organized, simple and easy-to-use way.

"Being positive is the only option".
- Subodh Gupta

"Everything you do, makes a Difference, and you must decide what is the Difference you want to make" —Dr. Jane Goodall

"Use the talents you possess, for the forest would be very silent, if only no bird sang except the best"-
Henry Van Dyke

1 LIVING GREEN

Environmental sustainability means living in harmony with nature, also referred to as living green. In order to achieve this, we first need to understand that the resources of the planet are not infinite, including the energy and the necessary raw material for everything we use every day. They are limited resources, and it is our responsibility to use them in such a way so that they remain available for future generations; that is *environmental sustainability*.

Everything we buy, every action, every decision we make, from the moment we get up in the morning until we go to bed, has consequences. This is known as the ecological footprint. It is the amount of resources used by each person. For example, when you buy food, you have to take into account the water and the land that was needed to grow what you eat. The ecological footprint also includes the energy that was used to grow it, to keep it refrigerated, the agrochemicals, the transportation, and many other factors.

Did you know, for example, that 240 gallons of water are needed to make a mobile phone? To produce one pound of meat, about 1,850 liters of water are used. To make a pair of jeans, 1,000 liters of water are required.[1] Some people use paper cups, so they don't have to

---

[1] Taikan Oki, Water Footprint, Institute of Industrial Science at the University of Tokyo, 2010

wash them, but the irony is that it takes over 2 gallons of water to make one coffee paper cup with a plastic lid.[2]

In this book you will learn many ways to reduce your ecological footprint, while increasing your quality of life and saving money! This concept of ecological footprint was developed in 1992 at the UN Development and Environment Conference. If the entire population consumed the same way we do in developed countries, we would need at least three planets to survive, so, as we will see later, the problem today is not overpopulation, but over consumption.

The **good news** is that the vast majority of ideas and ecological measures will also help you to save money and improve your health; significantly reducing your chances of getting diseases such as diabetes, cancer, heart disease, and other.

In this book you will learn what to buy and what not, you will also learn to read the labels carefully, so they do not deceive you. All this will contribute to your health and to the satisfaction of knowing that you are helping to leave a better planet for the next generations.

1.1 Reduce and Save!

In most occasions we buy for all the wrong reasons: because we are under stress, mad, bored, or maybe to be able to compete with others, for insecurity, or just for pleasure.

---

[2] What's in a Cup, Andrea Himoff, April 2016

Then we realize that objects do not fill the void we feel. On the contrary, they create complexity and conglomeration in our homes, which generates more stress and complication instead of a positive feeling.

When we learn to *live green*, we are not only part of the solution to climate change, but we also help our environment and our budget. An ecological economy is not only possible, but it is the only way to a better Planet, as we will see in greater  detail in chapter 10. All society, including inhabitants of other countries, benefits when we use resources thinking of others. In this book we will also take a look at the social impacts of Living Green.

1.2 Ecological and Renewable: the same thing?

Sometimes we confuse the terms *organic, ecological, renewable, and sustainable*, but in reality each one refers to a different concept. Let's see an example. Most of the papers used in schools and offices are made with trees that are 60 years old or older at the time when they are cut. This in principle is renewable because trees can be replanted and grown. However, the consumption rate is so fast that we do not give trees time to grow, thus promoting deforestation, and this is **not** sustainable.

On the other hand, hemp is a plant that grows wild, without the need to apply toxic agrochemicals to the soil, nor to be irrigated with water and at a very fast rate, so the hemp paper is renewable and sustainable.

Another example is the reuse of discarded materials such as car tires. To be ecological, we must consider that they are made of petrochemicals and therefore contain many toxins. We must consider this when reusing them, to determine the use that it will be given and avoid damaging the environment or our health.
To be environmentally friendly, old car tires can be used for potting ornamental plants, but not for edible plant gardens. It is good to choose plants that absorb toxins from the soil.

They can also be used for outdoor furniture, since the trees are able to absorb and clean the toxic gases they release into the air. But they should not be used inside, because they accumulate toxins and can cause respiratory diseases and allergies. We will discuss the definition of organic in the context of agriculture and food, in chapters 8 and 9.

1.3 Ancestral Wisdom

Most cultures in the Americas before colonization learned to live in harmony with nature. They used Earth's natural resources without eradicating them. They migrated to warm climate areas in winter and cultivated the fields in other seasons and regions, but they understood that the resources of the planet belonged to all species, not only to humans.

> We do not inherit the Earth
> from our ancestors ...
> We borrow it from our children."
> --- Native-American Proverb

Western culture didn't understand this and therefore saw the indigenous people as nomads, but in reality, they had winter and summer residences! Europe brought many good things to the "New World", but it also spread the notion that the human being has a dominating role over all other species; that all resources belonged to them.

After several centuries we have learned the hard way that resources are not infinite, and that, if we do not take into account nature, we cause terrible imbalance on it, which brings devastating repercussions previously unthinkable in other aspects of our habitat.

This book aims to make us realize again that all species are interdependent and that we all win when we respect, conserve, and restore the balance in Nature. We must understand that human beings are not above nature, but that we are part of it.

1.4 Green Health + Green Environment = Green $avings

There are many things we can do to make our lives more sustainable and benefit our planet, while reducing our ecological footprint. These simple measures will help you save thousands of dollars in electricity, water, gasoline, and other products, minimizing pollution and improving our quality of life.

For example, by avoiding disposable products, we save money, and decrease the volume of garbage in landfills. Therefore, the quality of water and air improve as it decreases the methane gas that is produced in landfills. We must bear in mind that this gas is 30 times more powerful in heating the atmosphere than carbon dioxide, CO_2. So just by doing this you will be saving money, decreasing pollution, and tackling global warming.

Later we will also learn about the toxins that many disposable materials infiltrate in our food supply. So, by avoiding them, you will also improve your health. We can reduce our waste to practically zero, thus achieving a more beautiful and healthier planet for all. Likewise, we can try to buy and/or use as little as possible, thus saving money and resources. Wouldn't it be nice to buy most of the products we purchase at a discount price? It's easier than you think! For example, most people use a lot more laundry or dishwashing detergent than actually necessary, as much as double the needed amount. The same goes for toothpaste. You only need a portion the size of a pea. By reducing the amount you use, you save! It's as if you always buy toothpaste and detergent at half the tag price! Another example: if you get used to printing all your documents using both sides of the paper, it is equivalent as if you always get your copy paper at 50% discount price!

It's a matter of habit: to live green is to change our consumption habits, so you also reduce your ecological footprint.

To lower our ecological footprint, we can also choose materials taking into account their impact on nature. For instance, if you are going to buy clothes, select products made with natural fibers instead of fabrics made with petroleum (such as polyester, microfibers, and nylon). Synthetic fabrics are responsible for as much as twice the greenhouse gases emissions, compared to natural fabrics. This is due to the production processes of the fibers and the cultivation process. Whenever you can, consider buying organic cotton. It is much softer than regular cotton and does not utilize any agrochemicals that augment climate change.

On the other hand, fabrics made of synthetic materials do not biodegrade. Nylon, for example, produces nitrogen oxide during its manufacture, which causes global warming.

In addition to that, according to scientific studies, synthetic fabrics accumulate more grease and therefore promote the development of odor-causing bacteria.[3] So, to smell better, maybe instead of a better deodorant, you just have to change the clothes you wear, especially for exercising!

Conventional (non-organic) fabrics use many agrochemicals, which can harm people, wildlife, bodies of water and the environment. Conventional cotton consumes approximately 1/5 of all pesticides (insecticides, fungicides, etc.) on the planet. In addition, it requires a huge amount of water to grow, more than 100,000 cubic feet of water per acre.

---

[3] Callewaert, C. et al., Microbial Odor Profile Of Polyester and Cotton Clothes after a Fitness Session, Appl. Environ. Microbiol. 2014, Nov. 80(21): 6611-6619

Everyday more and more eco-friendly fabrics are becoming available, such as bamboo, which grows rapidly by absorbing a lot of carbon dioxide from the atmosphere, without having to be watered and is naturally antibacterial. It also provides protection from the sun's ultraviolet (UV) radiation according to Dr. Tarannum Afrin and her colleagues at Deakin University in Australia.

Hemp fabric is usually organic since hemp naturally repels pests. It also protects you from UV rays and it is naturally antibacterial. It does not need an irrigation system. Other fabrics such as wool, jute, and soy are better options for the environment. Wool is naturally flame-retardant without the need for added toxic chemicals!

Did you know that hemp is one of the most versatile plants ever?

Below is a partial list of some of its many uses. Its scientific name is *cannabis*, hence the nickname or contraction 'canvas' for the fabric made of the fiber from the plant. Nowadays canvas fabric is usually made out of cotton, linen or vinyl, but in colonial times, all ropes, boat sails, wagon covers, and jeans were made with this material due to its strength and low cost. Some uses include:

- Food
- Paper
- Medicines
- Plastics
- Fabrics
- Beauty products
- Biodiesel fuel oil
- Ethanol gas
- Paints

In fact, the first draft copies of the constitution of U.S. were written on hemp paper, since it was commonly used at that time. (The final version is in parchment paper). Hemp is sustainable because it grows fast without damaging the planet. Hemp seeds are also very nutritious. They contain more omega-3 fatty acids than fish, which is why they are widely used by vegetarians and vegans.

Below are other examples of simple habits to gain **health, money and a better environment.**

- Clean your air conditioning filters weekly- it improves your health, eliminates impurities and fungi, and saves energy and money.

- Carpooling- it provides you with an opportunity to get to know your neighbors better and saves gasoline (See chapter 5)

- Walking or biking – they improve your health and also save gasoline.

- Consume local products- it benefits the local economy, which in the long run also improves your quality of life, saves money, and considerably reduces gas emissions due to the short distance required for transportation. (See chapter 8)

- Buy products with less packaging in non-individual family-size packages- it saves money and is less waste material that has to be thrown to the landfills or recycled.

- Use reused gift bags instead of wrapping paper or use recycled materials to wrap gifts – it saves money and resources.

- Use reusable water bottles (not plastic) - it avoids having to recycle, saves a lot of money and improves your health as discussed in Chapter 3.

- Buy products in dry or powder form if possible, such as soap bars, hair shampoo and laundry detergent. These are usually much cheaper and concentrated and since they weigh less, their ecological footprint in terms of transport is much lower.

- Recycle following the recycling rules of your municipality reduces the pollution of your environment and reduces the volume of your trash and therefore, trash collection fees, where applicable. (See chapter 11).

Every detail counts, the planet belongs to everyone, and we all gain health, money, and a better climate and environment.

In the following chapters you will learn many more ways to live green and improve your health and save thousands of dollars annually. And, best of all, you will be a positive contribution to building a better planet for you and the next generations to come.

2 CLIMATE CHANGE

... what it is and how it affects you.

Constant change: that's how we can describe the climate on Earth. However, when we talk about climate change, we refer to the new climate that we humans have created on this planet, due to the increase in emissions of what is known as greenhouse gases (GHG), produced by human activities.

These gases are so called because they have the capacity to absorb infrared (IR) radiation from the Sun in the atmosphere, which causes it to increase its temperature similar to the air inside a greenhouse used for plants, but in this case it is the whole planet, hence it's called global warming. So, the global warming of the planet causes the climate to change.

Examples of greenhouse gases are carbon dioxide, methane, and nitrous oxides. Gases used for refrigerants (air conditioners, refrigerators, etc.) are one of the factors that contribute the most to heating the atmosphere. They are between 1,000 to 9,000 times more powerful than CO_2 in absorbing IR (heat radiation).

Water spout at Mayagüez Bay, PR, September 2005.
Photo: Ricardo Ríos-Olmo

Some refrigerants, such as CFC and HCFC, were banned with the Montreal Protocol of 1987. In the year 2016, this protocol was amended to also prohibit HFCs beginning in 2019.

For thousands of years, since the last ice age, the level of carbon dioxide in the atmosphere was about 280 parts per million (ppm), but in 2018 it reached 410 ppm[4]. That is without taking into account other gases. The term CO_2e, is used to include the effect of all GHG besides CO_2, it means CO_2 equivalent. In order to stabilize the climate on Earth, we would need to lower the CO_2 concentration level to 350ppm, at most. According to the latest UN report (https://www.ipcc.ch/sr15/), we only have until 2030 to do this, before the point of no return.

Table 1. Warmest Years Recorded [Source: NOAA]

Global average over land and oceans [NOAA]

Order	Year	Anomaly °C	Anomaly °F
1	2016	0.94	1.69
2	2015	0.90	1.62
3	2017	0.84	1.51
4	2018	0.75	1.35
5	2014	0.74	1.33
6	2010	0.70	1.26
7	2013	0.66	1.19
7	2005	0.65	1.17
9	2009	0.64	1.15
10	1998	0.63	1.13

---

[4] www.noaa.gov/news/global-carbon-dioxide-growth-in-2018-reached-4th-highest-on-record

The hottest years ever recorded have been the most recent years as seen on Table 1 (Recorded since 1880)[5]. In fact, NASA[6] announced that the year 2014 was the first year since 1997 that ranked #1 on record despite not being a year of the El Niño phenomenon, which is really alarming. Then, 2016 broke all previous records.

Global warming is defined as the increase in the average temperature of the entire globe, both on the land surface and on the ocean. This causes changes in climate compared to the climate we have had for about 10,000 years since the last ice age. That is how global warming causes climate changes.

The consequences of this global warming are many: melting of the polar caps, rising sea levels, extreme events such as floods and droughts, extreme temperatures, both <u>colder</u> or hotter than normal, stronger storms and more common tornadoes, and their repercussions on public agriculture, health, and safety, among others.

---

[5] www.ncdc.noaa.gov/sotc/global/201513
[6] www.washingtonpost.com/blogs/wonkblog/wp/2015/01/16/its-official-2014-was-the-hottest-year-in-recorded-history/

The ice sheets continue to melt at the poles of the planet.

There are many myths about Climate Change and global warming, so it's important to clarify some [7]:

• Global warming is not a theory; it is a fact confirmed by science studies and thousands of scientists in over 130 countries.

• It has been happening for decades and it's already affecting millions of people, and it is intensifying

• The scientific consensus is that it is caused mostly by human activities, not by cycles of nature.

• Some of its consequences are irreversible and scientist say we must lower the concentration of greenhouse gases on or before the year 2030!

---

[7] An Inconvenient Truth: The Planetary Emergency of Global Warming and What We Can Do About It, Al Gore, Rodale Books, 2006

2.1 Scientific Evidence

The following graphs on the map of the world are from the Report of the Intergovernmental Panel on Climate Change (IPCC) of the United Nations (UN). These show the increase in average global temperatures over the ocean, land, and the sum of both for the last century, according to numerous scientific studies from around the world in multiple disciplines.

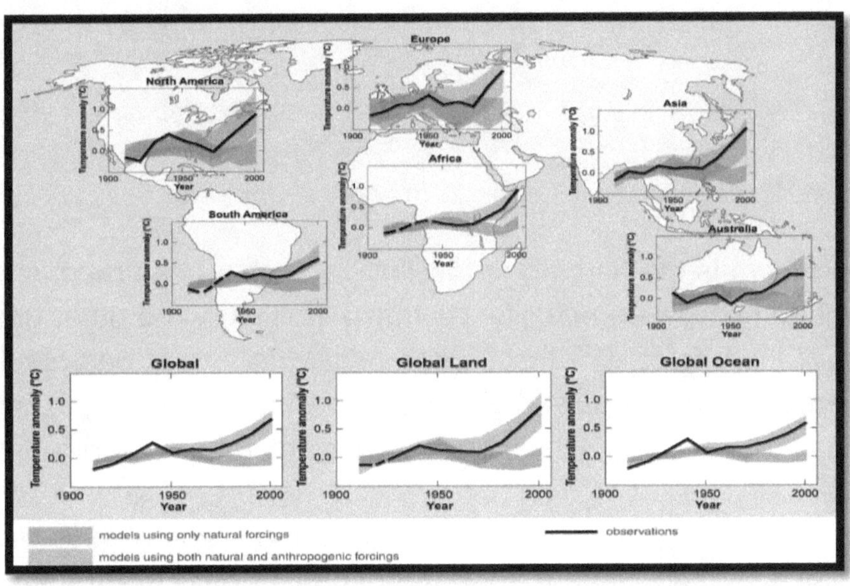

Increase in global temperature averages in the ocean, on land and the combination for the last century. Models that take into account only the natural cycles of the planet, models that also take into account human activities, and observations. Natural cycles alone DO NOT explain what is observed on the whole planet. (IPCC).

Some of these scientists, about 2,000, meet periodically at the UN, and form the IPCC. These graphs compare the scientific models that take into account only the natural cycles of the planet (in blue) and the models that also take into account human activities, i.e., anthropogenic factors (in pink) with the real measurements recorded in nature (in black).

As can be seen, natural cycles alone cannot explain what is observed in the entire planet! Therefore, it can be concluded that global warming is caused by human activities.

2.1.1 Human Activities

What are the activities that cause greenhouse gas emissions?

Among them is the burning of fossil fuels such as natural gas, coal and oil, to generate electricity. All these emit CO_2 and other gases, some of them toxic. For instance, mercury, is a toxic gas resulting from the burning of coal, and present in coal ashes. Mercury is known to cause biological defects in animals (including human animals).

Fossil fuels receive many subsidies from the US federal government which makes them appear cheaper than they really are. Fuel costs do not take into account external costs, that is, the costs of loss of health, pollution, and other consequences of their emissions, which we all end up paying.

Other examples of activities that impact the emission of greenhouse gases are transportation, the use of water[8], the fabrication of products (excessive consumption), and deforestation for construction and for agriculture. Incidentally, between 70 to 90% of the cereals that are grown are for feeding livestock, not humans. Landfills and livestock are sources of methane gas, a gas which is 25 times more capable than CO2 in trapping IR rays and, therefore, in absorbing heat (yet another reason to recycle and reduce waste). Likewise, in industrial agriculture many synthetic fertilizers containing nitrous oxides (NOx) are used. These are between 200 to 300 times more capable than CO_2 in heating the atmosphere and the planet. In addition, industrial agriculture uses pesticides that destroy the ozone layer, contaminate our environment, and damage our health.

The extremes: most people think that global warming will only cause high temperatures. But the reality is that global warming causes climate change and this in turn causes extremes in temperatures including intense colds. This is because climate change creates an imbalance in the natural cycles of the planet, which can affect things like the polar vortex and induce extreme winters.

---

[8] Water needs to be pumped and filtered to reach homes and buildings, and all that consumes energy that is responsible for greenhouse gas emissions.

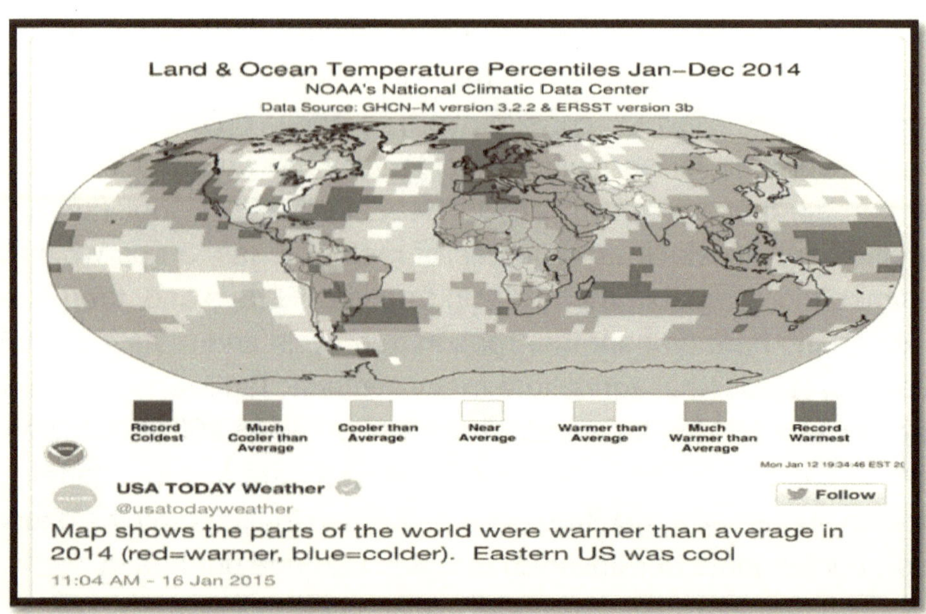

Warmer than average global temperature around the world for 2014, showing part colder than normal in purple.

The figure above shows the parts of the planet where warmer than normal temperatures were observed for the year 2014. It can be noted that there are regions that are colder than normal (shown in purple). This is also part of climate change. They are extreme due to the instability of climate caused by global warming.

2.2 All Kinds of Solutions

There are many solutions to curb climate change and, each country, each citizen, and each politician has to do his/her part. Among the solutions are to recycle, reforest, eliminate chemicals and agrochemicals that emit greenhouse gases, modify our diet, our consumption habits, conserve resources, eliminate disposable things, and find alternatives that coexist in harmony with nature having the least impact on the environment or ecological footprint. It is especially important to educate yourself on how to reduce our ecological footprint. Education is Power.

There is not a single magic solution, but you must look for a combination of several solutions, depending on the geography and circumstance of each country or region. Renewable energy could be part of the solution, but something that has more impact is to reduce. Reducing energy consumption means conserving energy. For instance, in the U.S. we use 4-6 times more energy per person than other industrialized countries such as Spain. We need conservation first in order to implement renewable energy in a cost-effective manner.

Sometimes nuclear energy has been portrait as a renewable energy when in reality it is not. It is an **alternative energy,** alternative to fossil fuels. However, nuclear energy presents too many risks especially for an island where there is nowhere to escape in the case of an accident such as Fukushima or Chernobyl. In the case of Puerto Rico, we must also recall that the island lies on a seismic zone, adding to the risks.

Organic agriculture, conservation, and diet modifications are other extremely important factors among the solutions to this global crisis and bring other benefits that we will discuss in this book.

This map shows how the coasts of Puerto Rico would be impacted due to sea level rise, if we continue business as usual. Source: http://www.floodmap.net using NASA data of 90 meters resolution from the SRTM (Shuttle Radar Topography Mission).

In this map you can see several municipalities that would be below sea level. Unfortunately, most of the population in Puerto Rico and the world lives on the coasts.

The impact would be very severe for everyone even for those who live in the center of the island because all the ports where the merchandise arrives are located on the coasts, and, therefore, a high percentage of the food we eat would be affected.

In addition to this, hurricanes, waterspouts that enter the earth becoming tornadoes, hailstorms, droughts, and floods will be increasingly common affecting life and property. Several researchers suggest that global warming may increase the number of eruptions

of volcanoes and the intensity of earthquakes across the planet[9,10],
This is because the heat is transmitted from the atmosphere to the
Earth and absorbed by the underground layers.

The island of Puerto Rico is close to several seismic faults which
makes it vulnerable to earthquakes and tsunamis. In fact, in Puerto
Rico on average there are more earthquakes weekly than in
California.

2.3 Ethical Aspects

Many of the continents where the effects of climate change have
been felt for decades in terms of environmental disasters, are
precisely the ones that produce less greenhouse gases and
consume the least. And that is the ethical and moral aspect of climate
change.

 It is our social and ethical responsibility to do everything possible to
reduce our impact on the planet as it is affecting more the people
who contributed less to our climate change. Many protests in
countries such as Kenya have been organized for precisely this
issue.

---

[9]www.alternet.org/newsandviews/article/560158/scientists_find_link_between_gl
obal_warming_and_earthquakes
[10]www.livescience.com/7366-global-warming-spur-earthquakes-volcanoes.html

2.4 Socio-Economical Aspects

The 2006 report by economist Sir Nicholas Stern concluded that global warming can cause the global economy to fall by 20%! This was summarized in an article from Times magazine in 2006.

This would affect us all and cause famine and even cause a collapse in the global economic system. We will elaborate on this on Chapter 10.

Another consequence of climate change is the increase in **diseases** due to the proliferation of mosquitoes, rats, and other animals that transmit viruses, losses in **agriculture**, lack of rain and **extinction** of animal species, such as the tree frogs, corals, vegetation, among others, because they cannot adapt so quickly to these changes.

The worst-case scenario that is seen in the scientific models, is the halt of the global oceanic belt. This oceanic belt is responsible for distributing the heat throughout the planet. This would have an effect similar to that presented in the movie "The Day After Tomorrow." In fact, this movie was based on a scientific report for its plot.

How could global warming cause this belt to stop? **As the poles melt, the salinity changes in the ocean, and, therefore, the density of the sea water also changes.**

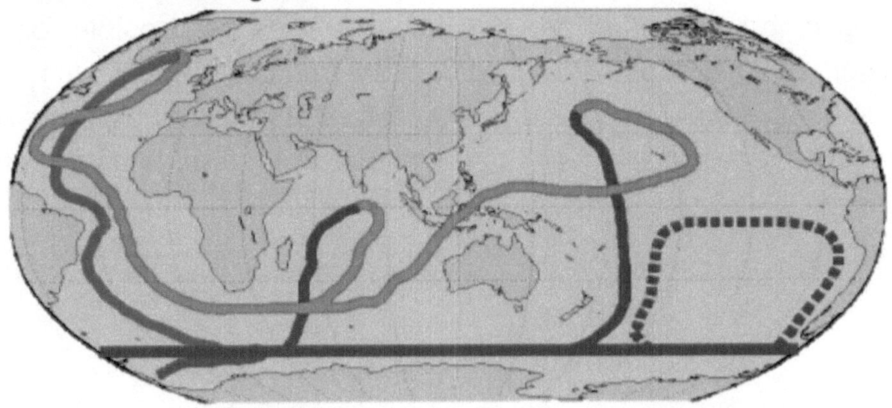

This causes the global oceanic belt to slow down and potential to stop, creating an ice age in Europe and the northern and southern hemisphere, and terrible heat in the tropics and the countries near the equator. [Source: IPCC]

Recent scientific studies, published in the journal Nature in April 2018[11] suggest that the oceanic belt has begun to slow down already. This is really alarming and could cause drastic changes in our climate.[12]

---

[11]www.carbonbrief.org/atlantic-conveyor-belt-has-slowed-15-per-cent-since-mid-twentieth-century
[12]https://e360.yale.edu/features/will_climate_change_jam_the_global_ocean_conveyor_belt

2.4.1   Coast Erosion

The greenhouse gases are not the only ones responsible for the erosion on the coasts. Excessive construction, especially in the maritime-terrestrial zone, causes disasters and loss of property and life. This, added to the rise in sea level and storms, is a recipe for disaster.

2.4.2   Storms

The 'tropical' storms have reached high latitudes up all the way to New York in 2012! This is well beyond the tropical areas of the world, where they used to be limited to. In fact, that same year, we had a hurricane season much higher than normal, with 19 storms (the average is 12) of which 10 became hurricanes (the average is 6). The hottest years on record, have occurred in the last 15 years. (See Table 1 above).

In 2004 the first hurricane occurred in Brazil, which is not normal for a latitude so far down from the equator [13]. Since 2014, the Weather Channel and weather.com are giving names to winter storms in the U.S..

In 2005, so many storms were formed that the names given in alphabetical order ended and it was necessary to resort to 6 Greek letters!

Year 2006 was a year of the event known as El Niño which decreases the number of hurricanes in the Atlantic. In 2010, the event known as La Niña occurred, which usually occurs 85% of the times after El Niño and increases the number of storms, but at the same time the jet stream moves up north to high latitudes and therefore storms tend to deviate to the north of the Caribbean and towards the East of the United States.

---

[13] What was Catarina? UCAR, 2005
https://www.ucar.edu/communications/quarterly/summer05/catarina.html

Amazingly, this sign shown above is not from the tropics but from Massachusetts, USA! If this trend continues, we will have to find another name for tropical storms, as they are proliferating at latitudes outside the Tropics.

2.4.3   World Population

Sometimes the growth in the world population is mentioned as one of the causes for climate change and for scarcity of resources. However, the truth is that if we face the fact that most of the world population lives without electricity and consumes very little, we can understand that in fact only a part of the population, in the most developed countries, is responsible for most greenhouse gas emissions.

In fact, planet Earth produces enough food to feed 10 billion[14] people and we are only 7 billion.

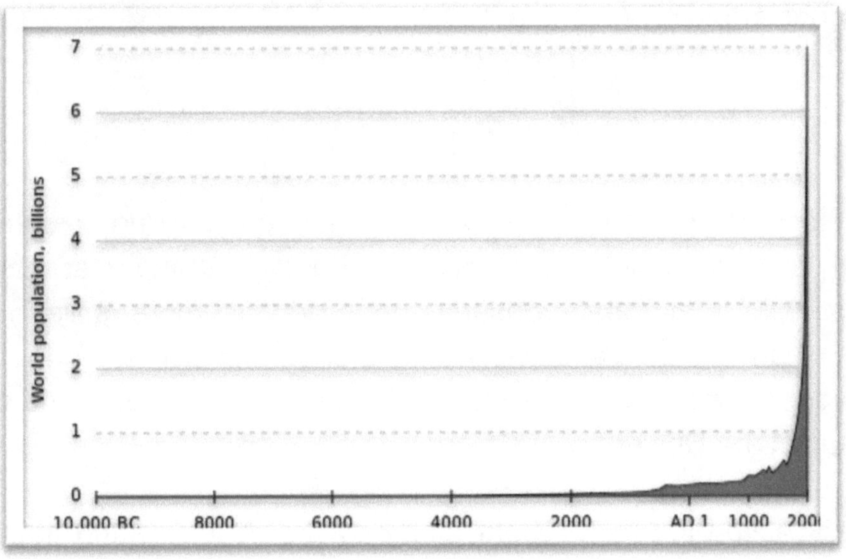

The figure above shows that it took the whole history of humanity to reach up to 1000 million (1 billion), in 1804. And then in just 200 years, in 2011, we have reached 7 billion.

The exaggerated consumption of goods, for example, electronic devices, produces a very detrimental impact on the planet and contributes highly to pollution. The appliances are designed to last less and less, to force people to buy more (this will be discussed in Chapter 6, and is known as planned obsolescence), and this causes greater waste of resources and landfill growth, in addition to recycling

---

[14] Holz-Gimenez at el., "We Already Grow Enough Food for 10 Billion People … and Still Can't End Hunger" , June 2012, Journal of Sustainable Agriculture 36(6):595-598

methods that affect the health of the inhabitants of the poorest countries. So, the problem is not overpopulation but overconsumption.

2.5 Best Kept Secret: Meat and the Environment

Most people know that the consumption of gasoline, electricity, water, and resources causes climate change. But the vast majority is unaware that meat consumption produces more greenhouse gases than all cars and trucks on the planet. This according to many science studies, including a report of the United Nations [15] and other studies at the University of Chicago[16].

In fact, according to a recent study by the World Watch Institute, more than half of the gases that cause global warming, 51%, are due to the production of meat for consumption[17]. This institute indicates that by the year 2050 either all humans are vegetarians, or we all perish for lack of water.

This leads us to touch up on the issue of the world population again. Our planet produces enough food to feed 2 to 20 times[18] [19] more people if they were all vegetarian! This is due to many factors

---

[15] UN News, "Rearing cattle produces more greenhouse gases than driving cars, UN report warns", 2006

[16] https://journals.ametsoc.org/doi/pdf/10.1175/EI167.1

[17] www.worldwatch.org/files/pdf/Livestock%20and%20Climate%20Change.pdf

[18] www.huffingtonpost.ca/2011/10/13/less-meat-save-world_n_1009056.html

[19] www.animalliberationfront.com/Practical/Health/robbins.htm

mentioned in chapter 4 of this book, including transportation, refrigeration, and agrochemicals used for cereals that feed these animals, among others. We will also see there that meat consumption causes several diseases, which, in turn, promotes the use of pharmaceutical drugs that are toxic to the environment.

In conclusion, if you want to be a positive contribution to the planet and leave a better planet to future generations, you do not have to buy solar panels or an electric car, it is sufficient that you change your diet, and in doing so, you will also improve your health.

In addition to the above-mentioned solutions, the governments must support a whole series of measures and legislation that contribute to lower our greenhouse gas emissions.

For instance, support local organic agriculture, improve recycling programs, make aggressive program to reduce the volume of our waste including banning single-use plastic and paper bags, re-institute reusable glass bottles for soft drinks (sodas), ban polystyrene (Styrofoam), establish deposits for plastic bottles, ban bottled water (except during natural disasters and emergencies, and even then, promote the use of water filtration systems, instead), continue with incentives for renewable energy, promote healthy ecological plant-based diet, make an aggressive plan to implement energy conservation measures, water, and other resources, review permit policies to maintain and restore coasts and green areas, educational campaign, among many other actions. We elaborate more about these topics on Chapter 9.

3   G REEN $AVINGS

This chapter focuses on the Conservation of all types of resources. A typical family of 4 can save between $1000 to $4000 annually by applying ecological measures. You will learn how to reduce the consumption of electricity and water, and waste generation by more than half, following some simple practices that I cover in this chapter. (In Chapter 6 you will learn ways to save money on gasoline). The advantage of Conservation is that it requires little or no initial investment.

3.1   Reduce your Water Bill

It is easy to understand that when we use gasoline, we are emitting greenhouse gases such as CO_2 which heat the atmosphere. Also, when we use electricity, we emit more or less amount of gases according to how that energy was generated; that is, the amount of gas emitted depends on whether it was generated by burning coal, oil, natural gas or using renewable energy. However, it is not so obvious to many people that the same happens every time we use other resources, such as water.

Every time we use water, we are also generating greenhouse gases! This is because of the energy required to pump the water to your faucet and the energy used for its treatment. We need to recall that, according to climate change models as documented in the United

Nations IPCC reports, drinkable water will be increasingly scarce due to climate change.

The documentary Blue Gold talks about the importance of water as an essential resource for life and how wars have already been unleashed due to water scarcity in some regions of the planet. This is an additional motivation to conserve water.

Thus, if we use less water, we will be helping the planet, lowering the amount of emissions into the atmosphere and saving money.

Figure 3.1 Dual-flush Toilet and other water-saving devices

If you install water-saving appliances such as faucets that use 0.5 - 1.5 GPM (gallons per minute), instead of 3-10 GPM, you will use less than half the water. These showers are designed so that the water comes out with force, in a way so that you do not even realize that you are using less. Similarly, if you install a dual-flush toilet which has two buttons, one for liquids and another for solids, the tank will use much less water. You will see your water bill reduced by about half and you recover the cost of these devices in a few months.

Another very economical option instead of acquiring a new double-flush toilet, is to buy a device that is installed inside the tank of a regular toilet. It does the same function. I installed mine in less than 10 minutes and Presto! you have a toilet that flushes the tank in one of the 2 water levels according to use. The device's cost is very low and hence, quickly recovered. It is also important to learn how to take short showers to save water. Two to three minutes is enough to shower efficiently. Close the shower while soaping, washing your hair or shaving.

Remember that in developed countries it is unhygienic to throw the toilet paper in the trash, because it ends up on the landfill and from there it can infiltrate into our rivers, creeks, and other bodies of water. Toilet paper should be flushed into the toilet since the municipal Aqueduct and Sewer Authority has the ability to treat the water and remove contaminants. But unfortunately, there are many myths. Some argue that toilet paper clogs the pipes, when in fact it is designed to dissolve in 30 to 120 minutes.

Another way to save money, related to water, and that greatly helps the planet, is to stop buying bottled water. Bottle water costs up to 10,000 times more than tap water, and the quality is similar depending on the region. In addition, bottled water is not regulated by the Water authority!

You can use a pitcher or a bottle with a filter (as shown on Chapter 11) if you do not like tap water or live in an area where water quality is questionable. There are stainless steel filters that work with gravity, so they do not need electricity to operate. They can filter heavy metals and even Nano particles. Did you know that many bottles and cans have an inner liner that contains Bisphenol-A (abbreviated BPA)? This chemical has been linked to type 2 diabetes, **obesity**, and other diseases because it mimics human hormones. [20] It has also been linked with immunodeficiency syndrome, multiple sclerosis, asthma, and allergies. [21]

---

[20] www.sciencedirect.com/science/article/pii/B9780128143070000396
[21] www.ncbi.nlm.nih.gov/pmc/articles/PMC5606650/

Some stainless-steel filters like Aquacera® work with gravity, so they do not need electricity to operate. They can filter heavy metals and even Nano particles.

In addition, almost all plastic bottles contain two other elements which also infiltrate into the water: antimony, and phthalates. Antimony has been linked to depression, and phthalate is also a hormone disruptor and has been linked to cancer. The best options are glass bottles or stainless steel. According to studies, the BPA substitute is as bad or worse than BPA itself, because it can cause hyperactivity and damage brain cells.

A Professor from Germany tested how the levels of antimony in water change due to it leaking from plastic bottles[22]. His results showed that the level of antimony rose considerably, from 2 ppt to 160 ppt (ppt stands for "parts per trillion"), after just several seconds of contact of the plastic bottle with the water. After 6 months, the level rose to 630 ppt. Remember that when you buy a bottle of water you do not know how long it has been stored. In addition, there are other factors such as temperature, freezing, and exposure to the sun, which could increase the amount of chemicals absorbed by the water from your bottle. So, all plastic bottles, even if they say "BPA-free", can have other chemicals leaking into your water or beverage.

BPA is also found on most store receipts and airplane boarding tickets since they're used as thermal paper coating[23]. Try to use digital versions, avoid touching and wash your hands to minimize exposure.

---

[22] Shotyk,W. et al., Antimony in recent, ombrotrophic peat from Switzerland and Scotland: Comparison with natural background values and implications for the global atmospheric Sb cycle, Global Biogeochemical Cycles, Vol. 18, 2004

[23] Minnesota Pollution Control Agency https://www.pca.state.mn.us/green-chemistry/bpa-thermal-paper#strategies-66f00276

A simple way to use less electricity from air conditioning is to look for ways to acclimatize your home's temperature without using energy. For example, planting trees that provide shade in the summer to the bedrooms in the afternoon can lower the temperature by up to 10° Fahrenheit (5° Celsius). As an added bonus, having trees in your landscape usually increases the value of your property. Trees also reduce greenhouse gas emissions by absorbing CO_2. In Puerto Rico, the Natural Resources Department gives up to 200 free trees per family. This is also true in many other communities.

We must always be aware that every time we turn on any electrical device or even a lightbulb, we are emitting greenhouse gases and contributing to global warming. In Puerto Rico more than 95% of electricity is generated with fossil fuels as of 2017. Law 82 of 2010 established that Puerto Rico must generate 15% of renewable energy by the year 2020. This goal is very low compared to other countries whose goal is to produce between 80 to 100% of electricity using renewable energy. In Puerto Rico, being an island that imports all its fuel from the outside, it makes even more sense to use the sun, wind and/or waves to generate energy. But before considering renewable energy, we must realize something much more important: conservation.

Figure 3.2 Image showing light pollution with data provided by Marc Imhoff from NASA GSFC and Christopher Elvidge from NOAA NGDC. Source: Craig Mayhew y Robert Simmon, NASA GSFC.

If you look at this nocturnal image of the world taken from a NASA satellite, you will realize that our island shines bright, much more than most other countries. In fact, electric power is wasted in Puerto Rico. There are too many lights at night in public and private places. This provides a false sense of security.

There are more efficient ways to be safe, such as installing night cameras, motion sensors, or buying a watchdog. Furthermore, in most streets you do not need so much lighting. In countries like Spain, they use 4-6 times less electricity per person and the quality of life is the same as in Puerto Rico or maybe even better! So, keep in mind that before considering installing a solar system in your home it is essential that you focus first on conservation. You can lower your consumption by at least 50%. In my case I lowered my bill to ¼ part of what I used to consume, before installing solar panels, as we will see later.

There are many other types of renewable energy, for example, biomass, which uses waste from animals and plants to produce energy. In this case, the energy is produced when organic matter is decomposed or burned. It carries risks of contamination of water and air, if it is not done correctly. There are also several types of solar and wind energy which will be discussed in Chapter 4.

Figure 3.3 Meters for monitoring electrical consumption of appliances

To see how much your electricity consumption is, you can buy one of several meters available. They tell you the amount of power, voltage, current, and other electrical variables, your devices are consuming. They even tell you how much money you are spending if you enter the value of the current energy cost of your country.

Another simple way to save energy is to disconnect all appliances when you do not use them. For example, cell phone chargers use between 70-95% of the energy even when they are not charging your cell phone. This is known as *phantom loads*. They are the energy consumed by the appliances when they are turned off but remain connected.

The same can be done with computers, not leaving the adapter or transformer connected as most designs continue to use energy as if they were charging the laptop. You can notice this energy expenditure if you touch the transformer box, and it feels hot. You are paying to generate that heat.

And very often, we have the printer, and many appliances connected all the time even though they are used very sparingly. Get used to disconnecting them, especially when you're not in the office and during weekends or if you're traveling.

Why do appliances still use electricity even when they are turned off?

The secret is in what we call transformers, which are basically 2 coils inside the black boxes that are in the devices' connector cables. Their function is to change the voltage from the level out of the the power outlet (110 volts) to the level that your device needs.

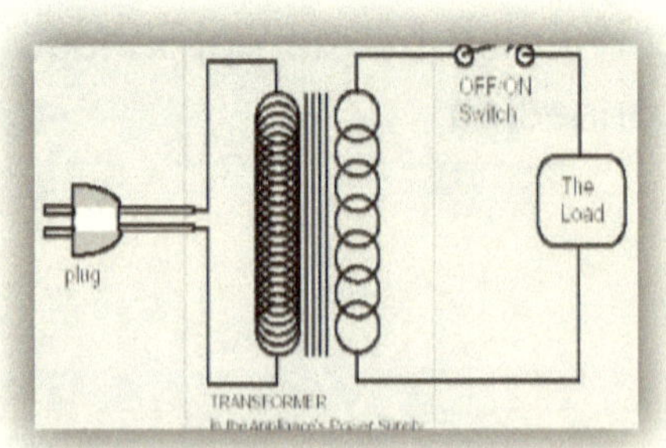

The reason is that the transformer consists of two circuits or closed loops that conduct electric current and even if you turn off the electric device, the loop that is connected to the wall is still closed and therefore it continues to waste energy while it is connected. There are exceptions with some transformers designed so that they do not have phantom loads.

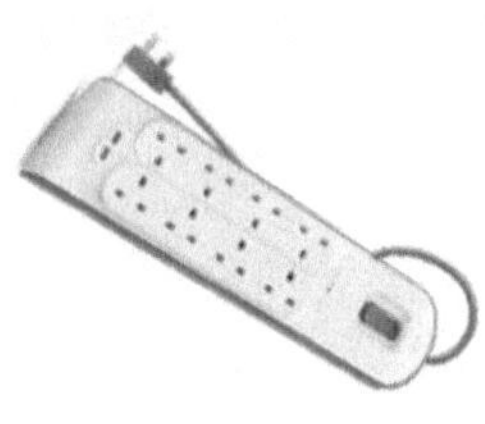

In some electrical equipment there are also components that store energy and are continuously charging and discharging, all this contributes to the so-called phantom loads. The easiest way to avoid having to keep connecting and disconnecting the appliances, is to get a multi-connector (or smart strip) and connect them all to it. In this way, you do not have to disconnect anything, simply turning off the multi-connector is equivalent to turning them off all at once. Another myth: some people might tell you that you should not disconnect appliances such as water heaters because they can be damaged, this is a not true. In most cases, you can save energy turning it on only when used. Try it.

In the following graph, let's look at the different types of lightbulbs commercially available and their *real cost*. The real cost is the sum of the initial cost plus the cost of operation. The incandescent bulbs (top line on the graph) have a lower initial cost, but it ends up being much more expensive due to its operating costs. This shows that sometimes what appears to be cheap is actually more expensive on the long run. In addition, the LED bulbs (green line on the graph) and fluorescent bulbs (orange line on the graph) do not emit much heat.

Therefore, when you go shopping for a lightbulb (or anything for that matter), do not look only at its initial cost, but also take into account what you will pay for its operation. This way you will realize the real cost of things. The LED bulb is the cheapest one in the long run and the incandescent turns out being many times costlier because it consumes 10 times more electricity.

In addition to this, LEDs do not contain mercury like fluorescents do, so they do not pollute, and you don't have to pay to dispose of them. If you do have to throw away a CFL, remember to dispose of correctly (the least you can do is to wrap it on a bag or enclosure before throwing in the trash can). Another advantage of LED lightbulbs is that they do not get too warm, so they do not heat your home, adding to air conditioning costs during the summer.

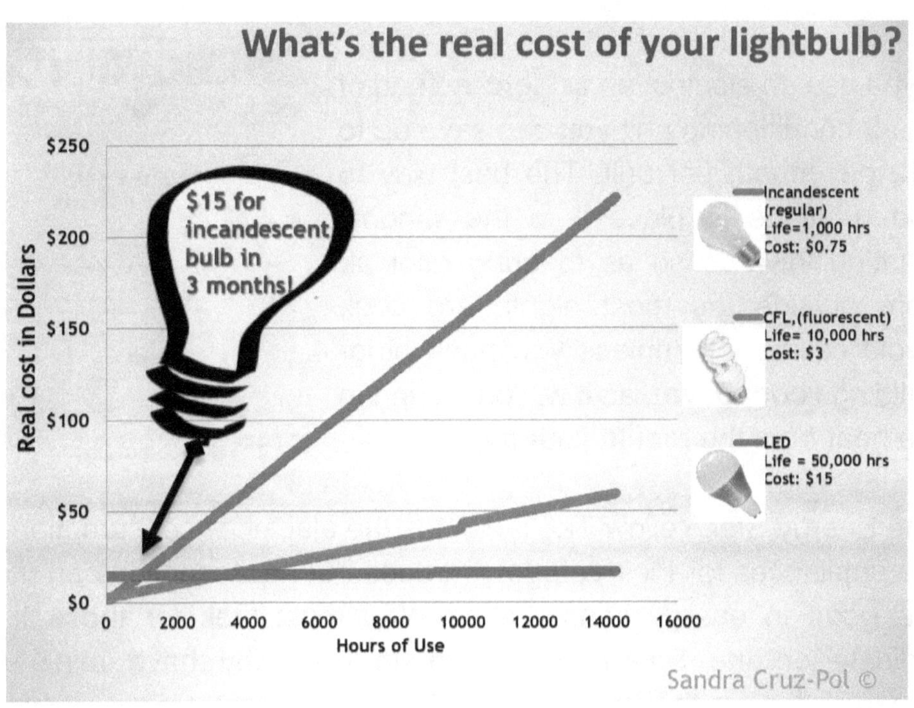

If you use an air conditioner unit, set it to 76-78° Fahrenheit (25 Celsius), so the room is cool, not frozen. Wear cool clothes instead of jackets or sweaters. Dress according to the weather forecast. All this will help save us from unnecessary CO_2 emissions, refrigerants, and other gases that pollute the atmosphere and damage the ozone layer.

If you use an electric fan at night instead of an air conditioning unit you can save up to $12 per month per unit. The best way to use a fan is to place it in the window pointing inwards so as to bring cool air from outside, as most nights are cool. Avoid ceiling fan (unless you have other building floor above), as it will only bring in the heat from the roof to your room.

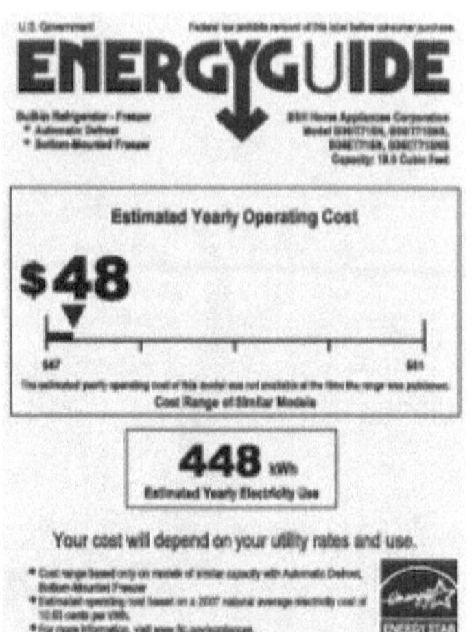

The Energy Star Yellow Tag indicates the electricity consumption of the appliances for their category, it does not necessarily mean they are good in energy conservation. You must look for those that indicate on the Energy Guide rating that they have minimum consumption for their category. Choose those that are as close as possible to the left side of the scale. That will make a big difference in your monthly energy bills and means lots of savings.

Solar heaters are an excellent investment, usually recovered quickly though electricity bill savings. They last for decades and save between $20 - $70 per month. Just remember to clean the solar panels annually with a mixture of white vinegar and water (1: 4) and to remove dust to improve their efficiency.

Another alternative is to use gas appliances, such as a gas cloth dryer and a gas stove range. They save between $15- $40 per month and are less harmful to the planet because they generate less greenhouse gas emissions.

You can also hang clothes in the sun the old-fashion way and save a lot more. If you live in a place where it rains every day, you can hang clothes under a roof as in a terrace.

Instead of using an electric iron, you can iron with vinegar! Mix a cup of water and 1/3 cup of white vinegar in a spray bottle. You can add a few drops of essential oil such as lavender, if you wish, but do not worry about the smell of vinegar, as it disappears as soon as the garment dries. In about 5 minutes you will see the wrinkles disappear from the clothes! As an added bonus, vinegar kills the bacteria that cause the bad smell.

If we apply some of these simple concepts at home, we can help curb Global Warming while saving money.

Let's see as an example how I lowered my electric energy. The savings are even larger because the cost of electricity in Puerto Rico is about double than the average in the U.S.

Next picture shows my typical energy bill, for a family of four adults. For close to 1400 kWh (kilowatt-hours) of electricity we paid $260. It was not uncommon to have monthly bills of over $300! This is with no central air-conditioner system in a Caribbean Island.

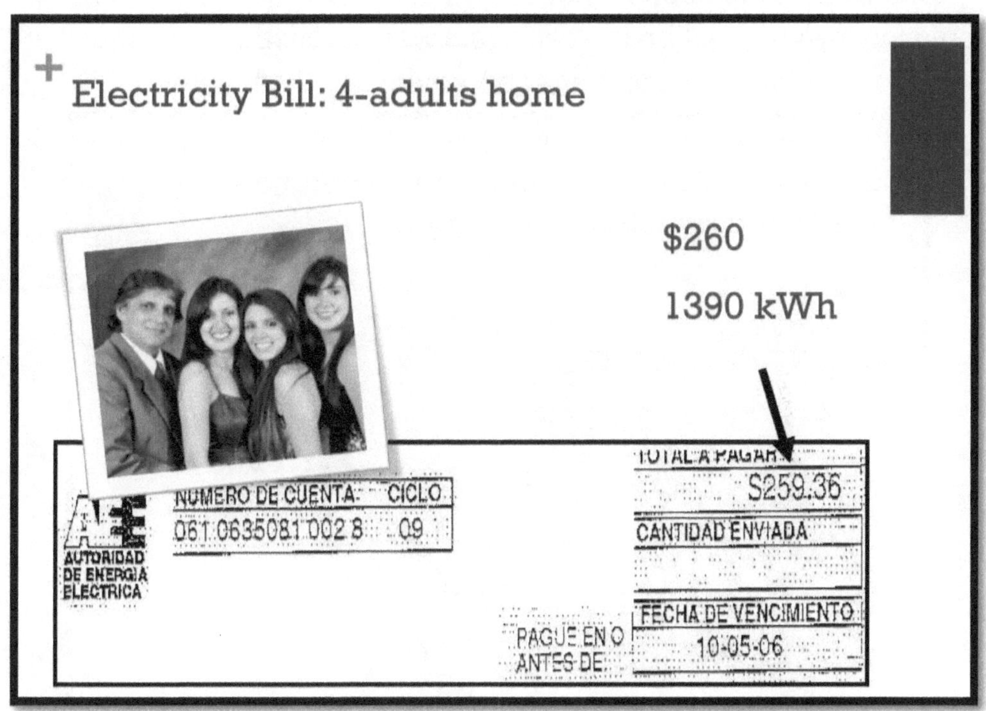

Then I started to apply ecological measures in order to help the planet. After eliminating phantom loads and switching some incandescent bulbs for CFL or LED, the next-month bill went down to 1160 kWh, a savings of almost $70. This is equivalent to a saving $840 per year. But this was only the beginning.

Next month, after using electric fans instead of air conditioners, we managed to half the bill compared to just 2 months earlier! Our bill came for less than 700 kWh, at a cost of $113. The nights in Puerto Rico are usually cool, but houses are in general poorly designed, with low ceilings and little ventilation, so they keep the midday heat trapped inside the house. That's why I placed the fans in the windows pointing inwards, not on the ceilings. I was surprised to find that it felt like having air conditioning after approximately just 1 hour.

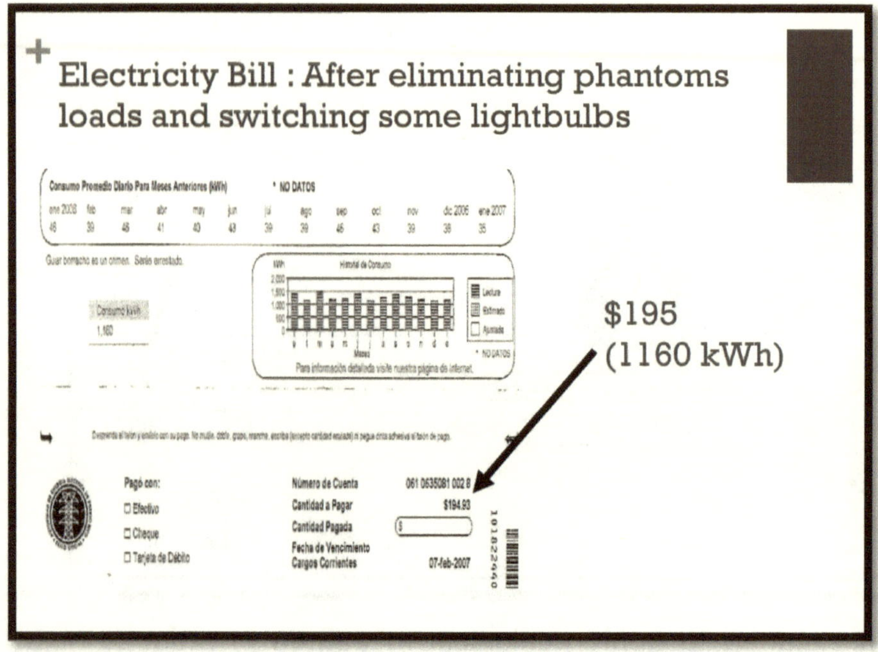

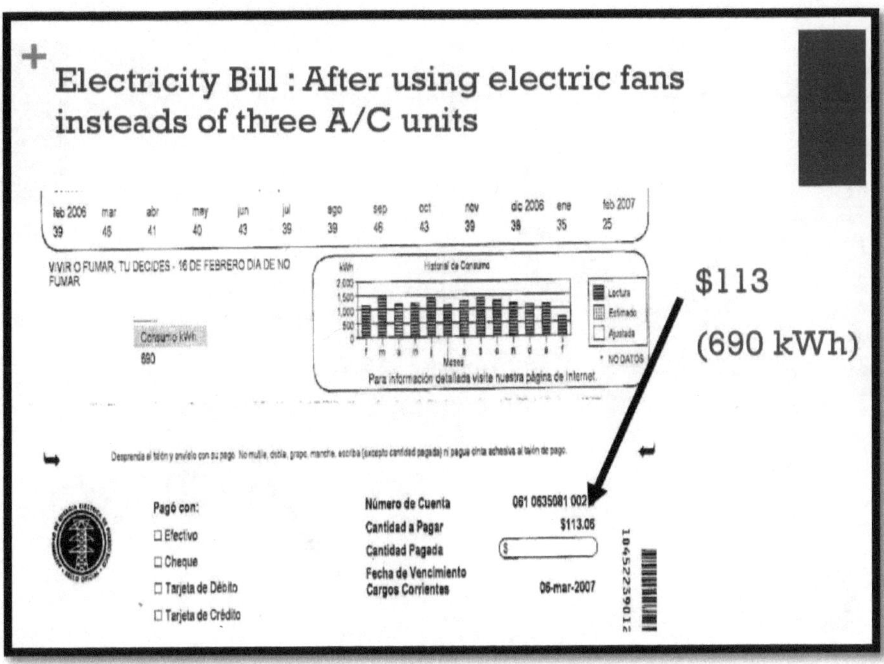

After installing a solar water heater, the bill went down even more at only 400 kWh at a cost of $74. This is equivalent to an annual saving of 12 x (260-74) = $ 2230. Not bad, right?

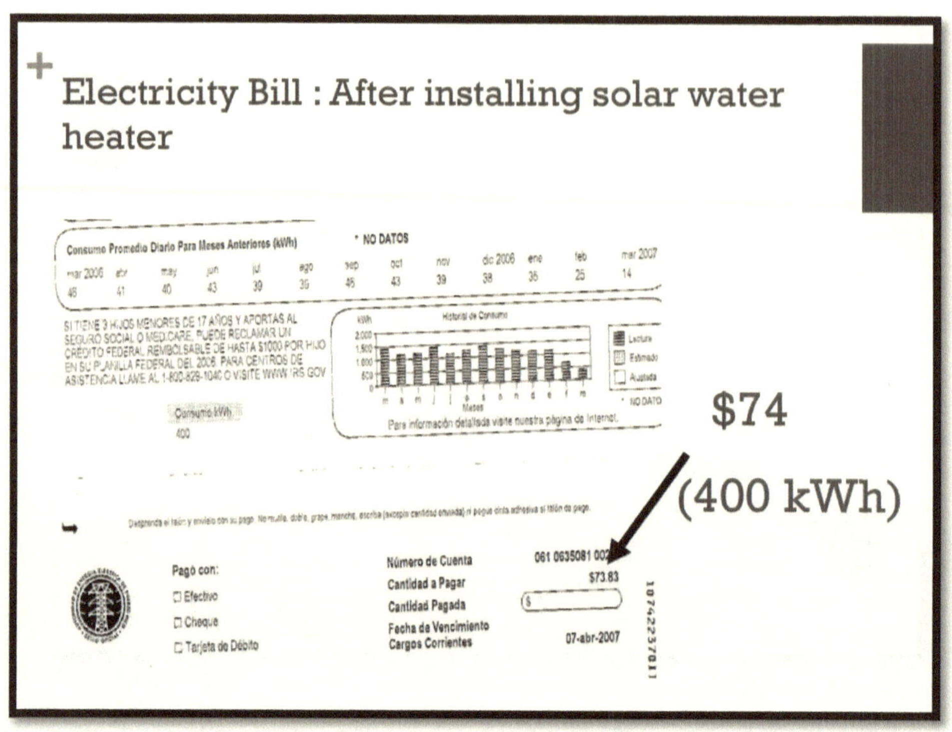

In summary, electricity consumption first went down from 1400kWh to 400kWh for an average saving of $2230 per year (based on electricity costs in Puerto Rico in 2004). All these economic savings are also ecological savings, so we all win.

After all this, we installed a gas cloth dryer, gas stove, and the bulbs were all changed to LED. Our energy bill was further reduced to only 270 kWh at a cost of only $55, for an estimated savings of over $3000 annually.

In the U.S. a family of 4 can easily save over $1,500 annually by applying only energy measures. This without counting the savings on your water bill and others.

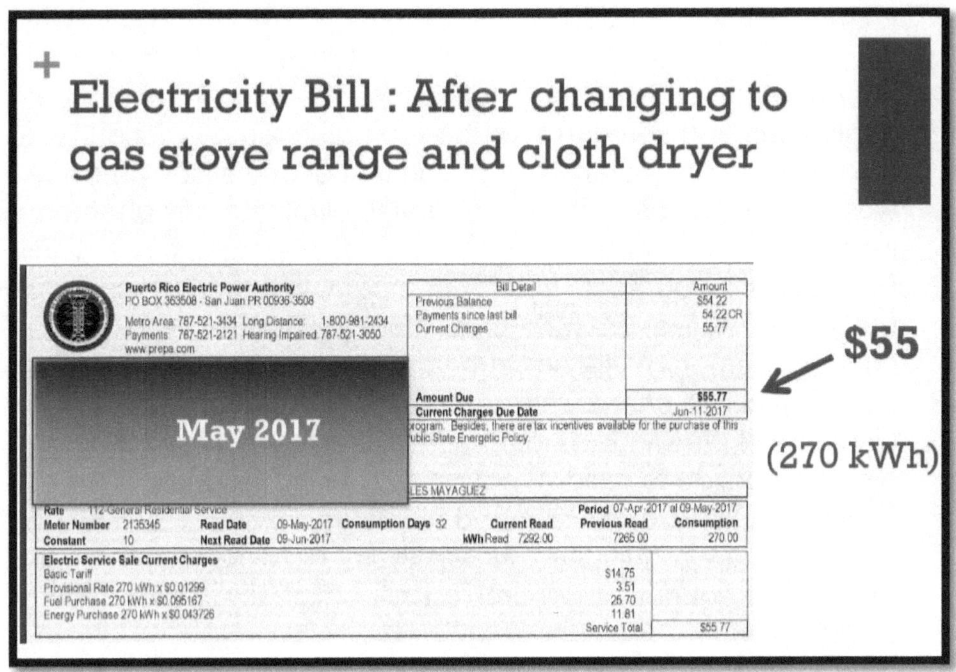

In addition, you will have the satisfaction of doing your part to help reduce greenhouse gases that heat the atmosphere causing climate changes that affect the lives of so many animal species, including humans, creating a better planet for your children and nephews.

To summarize, I present below several simple measures to save and help the environment. Most have none or low initial costs, but if they do, the costs are quickly recovered in savings:

1. Kill Phantom loads - use a multi-connector to connect several appliances and you can turn them off all at once. Disconnect the breakers of appliances that you do not use all the time like washing machines. This way you also eliminate any phantom loads from these appliances.
2. Find out with your local energy company whether the price of the electricity varies with time of day. For instance, if it's cheaper from 9pm till 6am, run your dishwasher after 9pm.
3. Disconnect cell phone chargers, printers, and computers.
4. Use fans in the windows during the summer months (bringing air from outside to inside), not on the ceiling (except for lower floors in multi-level houses and buildings).
5. If you use air conditioners, keep them at 76-78°F and clean the filters frequently to optimize their efficiency. Keep heater at 65°F in winter months.
6. If you have a line telephone, use a corded one instead of a wireless, they don't need power to work.
7. Read and compare Energy Star® labels and choose the smallest appliance and the lowest consumption for your needs.
8. Install infrared sensors in the rooms where the bulbs are usually left on.
9. Hang clothes outdoors to dry if possible.
10. Consider gas appliances, such as stove and cloth drier.
11. Acquire a solar water heater.

12. Choose an LCD LED TV and buy the smallest size you need.
13. Choose laptop over desktop; it uses about 1/3 the energy compared to a typical desktop and do not require battery backup which uses up additional energy since they must remain on all the time. Check your specific model energy use rating.
14. Use a pressure cooker (stainless steel, not aluminum) to shorten cooking time. Use iron skillet, cooks at low or medium heat setting. Both save energy.
15. Avoid using more than one refrigerator or freezer in your home. The energy you pay is much more than the savings of buying frozen family packages.
16. Use LED light bulbs (Light-emitting diodes). If you use CFL, remember to correctly dispose of them when they fuse because they contain mercury. Do not throw them in the trash, wrap them in a strong plastic bag or bag.
17. Use rechargeable batteries and remember never to throw any type of battery into the trash as they may contain heavy and toxic metals that pollute our environment.
18. Use a mobile smartphone App for TV Remote Control. This way you avoid the need to replace batteries in your remote controller. This requires a phone with IR capability.
19. Plant trees that provide shade to your home's bedrooms in the summer. This can lower the electricity bill up to 10%. (Consult with Natural Resources the type of trees so that their roots do not damage your home structure).
20. Apply a reflective treatment on the ceiling to keep your home cool.
21. Consider renewable energy for your home (wind turbines, solar photovoltaic or other).

We are not trying to save the planet. The planet is not at stake here. If we pollute and continue to change the climate, the ideal conditions to allow life as we know it will change, bringing natural disasters, floods, and unimaginable consequences for many. But still the planet would not end; the planet has all the time in the world. It will wait and adapt, and perhaps another kind of life will emerge at some point, even if it is millions of years after an environmental chaos.

In short, if we continue to abuse natural resources it is us who are in danger of extinction, ourselves, homo-sapiens, and many other species, not the Planet.

3.3 More Savings

Contrary to popular believe, it is not cheaper to buy a new printer than to buy ink. Actually, what very few people realize is that new printers come with almost empty cartridges!

It is much more economical to buy a new cartridge because they come with a lot of ink. This is a common mistake because almost nobody reads the number of milliliters of ink contained in the cartridges. It is written on the package.

3.4 Reducing the Size of Digital Files

Most people think they help the planet by sending email instead of paper documents. However, this is not always the case. You can help the environment and yourself by learning tricks that will reduce the size of the files on your computer.

It is easy to understand that printing on paper uses energy from cutting, processing, and transporting trees. But did you know that electronic messages also consume energy? In fact, unsolicited e-mail messages in the US are responsible for a sufficient energy consumption to power over 2.4 million homes during a whole year! This is equivalent to the emissions of greenhouse gases from 3.1 million cars[24]. This is why it is important to think twice before sending an unnecessary or too large email (photos, documents, etc.).

Emails represent a use of energy that causes emissions of gases that heat the atmosphere. Unsolicited email messages in the US and PR are responsible for a sufficient energy expenditure to power over 2.4 million homes for a whole year. Reduce the size of your emails.

---

24 McAffee, "Spam Impacts The Environment, Not Just Your Business",http://resources.mcafee.com/content/nacarbonfootprintspam

For example, every time you read and delete a single email (such as the so-called Junk or Spam mail), an average of 0.3 grams of CO_2 is emitted into the atmosphere, equivalent to driving a car for 3 feet. This varies with several factors such as the size of the file, the type of connection, the type of computer, the server that stores and processes the messages, etc.[25] According to the French Agency for Environment and Energy Management (ADEME), professional emails emit the equivalent of 13.6 tons of CO_2 every year.[26,27]

Sending emails is still a better alternative than printing paper in terms of environmental impact, as long as we use it correctly and with moderation. If you are going to print, use both sides of the paper.

3.4.1　How can we help the Planet when we send emails?

Use Unsubscribe services to stop receiving messages of no interest to you, instead of blocking them. Blocking them or sending them to your Trash folder keeps them on the server, taking up space and

---

[25] Google, "Green Computing: Efficiency At Scale", http://static.googleusercontent.com/external_content/untrusted_dlcp/www.google.com/en/us/green/pDfs/google-green-computing.pdf , 2011

[26] Vita Sgardello, "The True Impact of Email", www.earthtimes.org/scitech/true-impact- Email/1147/ , Earth Times 2011

[27] Audrey Garric, "Web Surfing, Email and Memory Downloads Take An Environmental Toll", www.guardian.co.uk/environment/2011/aug/02/carbon-emission-emails-computing-garric, The Guardian, UK, 2011

energy. Empty your Trash email folder regularly and remember to cancel unwanted subscriptions.

Do not re-send chain messages you receive. More than 99% of messages asking for help, such as *'Lost girl of a known friend'*, *'if you do not send this you do not have a heart'*, *'if you send this message, they will donate 3 cents to ...'*, etc., are false. You can corroborate their veracity by doing a search with the title of the message in several websites such as http://urbanlegends.about.com or www.snopes.com.

Or simply, delete them immediately without sending them forward. This is how we stop these chains from propagating.

The reality is that they send these messages in order to capture your email address and that of your friends, and then sell the list of these emails to cyber merchants. Next you start receiving more unsolicited emails from alleged princes, from miraculous chains, from offers, etc.

Another way to help reduce your email-footprint is to avoid sending large messages (with documents of 500kB or larger in size). When receiving a presentation or file too large, consider one of these options below.

3.4.2 Options to reduce the size of emails

Often the presentations you receive are already available on the web. Do a search on the Internet with a service like Google, Yahoo, or Blackle, and if you find it already on the web, then send only the link. This will make the size of your email about 100 times smaller, thus saving energy, time, storage resources on the server and communications bandwidth.

If the presentation is not on the internet, use a free service to upload the presentation to the internet, and send only the link. This will also make the size of your email much smaller. Examples of free services for this purpose are: www.yousendit.com or www.sendspace.com, Dropbox, or an FTP service (File Transfer Protocol)[28] .

Avoid sending messages with medium files (smaller than 500KB but larger than 100kB) if they are addressed to more than one person. When you send to multiple recipients, the effect is multiplicative. That is, if you send a message of 100kB to 7 people, it is like sending an email of 700kB.

---

[28] Master New Media
www.masternewmedia.org/how_to_send_large_files_without_email

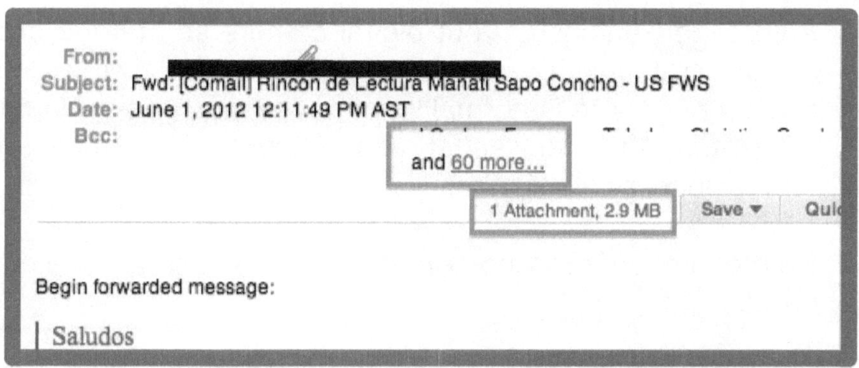

Figure 3.5 Giant messages like this one use up many resources including energy, time, server disk space and communications bandwidth. In this example a message of 2.9MB was sent to 65 people. This is equivalent to 188MB!

Yet another way to help reduce your email-footprint is to **Compress** the files you send.

3.4.3 How to Compress digital files:

- In documents like MS Word, select Format> Pictures> Compress All

- Use photos in .jpg or .gif formats and avoid using the Bitmap format (i.e. .bmp)

- Use programs to create .zip files

- To send photos by email, use free services which do not lower the resolution of the photos, or Facebook and again send only the link.

- Adjust the Settings of your digital camera so that the photos are generated with a size of 500kB instead of 1MB or more. Such a huge size is normally not necessary, unless you want to capture the freckles in your pictures ☺ or you are a professional photographer.

- Delete from your mailbox (Inbox) all the messages you do not need.

- Do the same with the garbage box (Trash, Spam, and Junk); you should empty them often because storing them on the server consumes energy. Some email services provide a setting where you can choose to have the messages deleted after a specific time of being in the Trash.

In summary, all resources must be used as what they are: finite, limited resources, including emails. This is why it is essential that you always consider whether it is really necessary and vital to send each message, and when it's a large size, you should reduce it using some of the approaches listed in this section.

You will be saving energy, time, resources, and what is more important: you will be reducing the amount of greenhouse gases that are emitted into the atmosphere, thus slowing global warming and climate change. It's simple, it's just a matter of habits.

4 RENEWABLE ENERGY

Every day, solar energy, wind and other renewables that have minimal impact on the Planet become more accessible to all.

Renewable energy is defined as energy that uses sources that do not run out, contrary to fossil fuels (coal, petroleum oil and natural gas), which are limited resources on the planet.

All forms of energy generation have some environmental impact, as shown on the next graph. However, the environmental impact of renewable energy is much lower than that of fossil fuels and nuclear energy, which cause many emissions of greenhouse gases and use a lot of water to cool their boilers, respectively, thus affecting fish and other marine life. In addition to this, they have social impacts and terrible risks from potential spills and accidents.

GHG (CO$_2$e lbs/kWh)

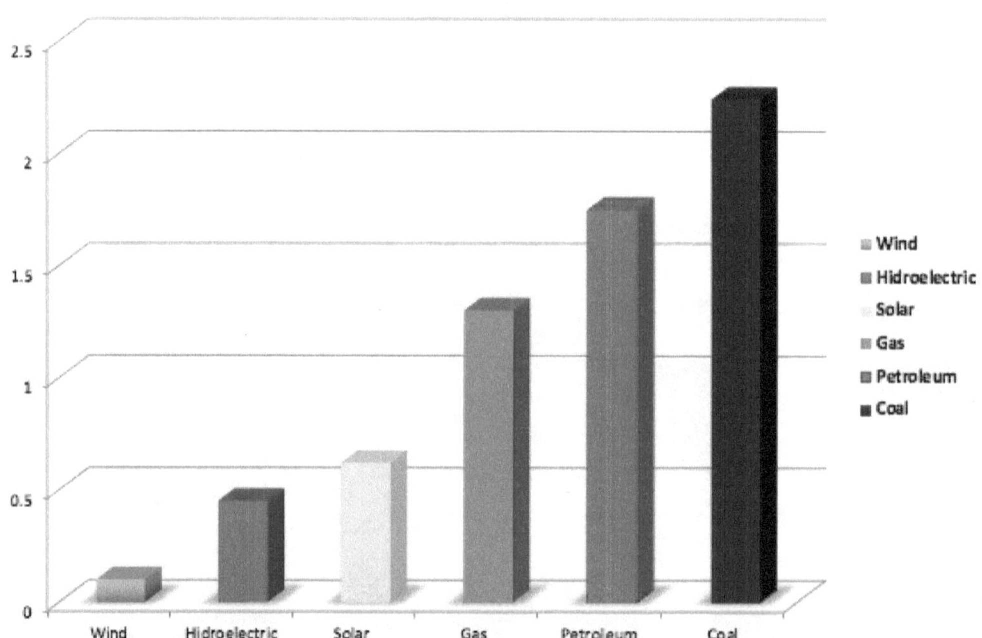

Figure 4.1 Environmental impact of various forms of energy generation in terms of the amount of emissions generated (CO$_2$ equivalent) per kilowatt hour (KWh) of energy. In the case of nuclear energy, the impacts are on the ecosystem and use of water as explained in this section.

4.1 Types of Renewable Energy

The types of renewable energy available on each region of the world depend on its specific geographic condition. In the case of the island of Puerto Rico, there are wind, solar, and ocean energy. Nuclear energy is not renewable, because uranium is limited on the planet and also carries with it many risks as has been shown historically in numerous accidents in Japan, Russia, and the U.S. These countries are much larger, and in case of an accident they can evacuate their population to other cities. Puerto Rico, being a small island, would have nowhere to go in case of an accident.

4.1.1 Wind Energy

Wind or eolic energy uses wind to move turbines which contain magnets and windings that generate an electric current when they move. Conventional wind turbines are as pictured on the image above.

Vertical turbines are a more viable alternative for many regions with than conventional turbines because they can be installed on roofs and small spaces. Vertical turbines can operate efficiently with low wind. Moreover, they do not kill birds because they rotate slowly. There are even some innovative designs of wind turbines no blades[29].

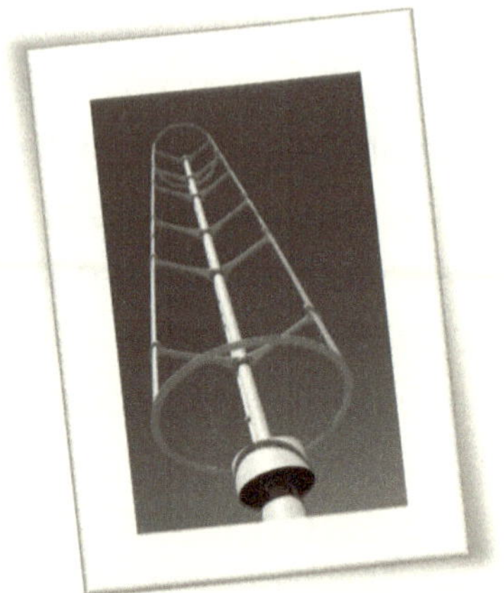

At this point I must clarify that, according to studies, conventional wind turbines are responsible for far fewer deaths of birds than domestic cats in a ratio of 4: 2000. Estimates published on 2013[30] state that wind farms killed approximately 20,000 birds in the United States in 2009 but nuclear plants killed about 330,000 and fossil fueled power plants more than 14 million.

In Puerto Rico there are regions with enough wind to make wind energy cost effective as shown in the following map. The areas with orange and red are the zones with enough wind for turbines to be cost effective.

---

[29] www.wired.com/2015/05/future-wind-turbines-no-blades/
[30] Sovacool, (Jan 2013), *"The avian benefits of wind energy: A 2009 update"*, Renewable Energy 49: 19-24.

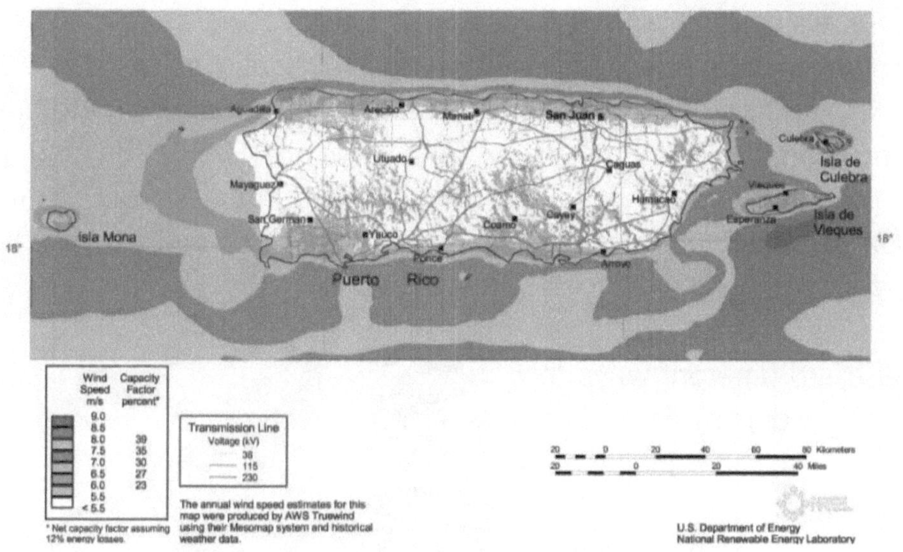

Average annual wind speed over Puerto Rico

Another advantage of these vertical turbines is that they resist wind gusts and are less noisy than conventional wind turbines.

4.1.2 Solar Energy

There are many types of solar energy. For example, solar thermal concentrates sunlight using mirrors to heat water that moves turbines with its steam to generate electricity. Another type uses solar panels that have the ability to convert solar energy into an electric current. This is known as photovoltaic (PV) energy. Usually when we talk about solar energy, we refer to the latter.

There are several options to acquire a photovoltaic system, such as companies that offer contracts where they lease or rent the solar system and pay for it in several decades. Others allow you to buy it in installments. Remember that it is always cheaper, in the long run, to buy instead of leasing. You will save even more if you pay it as soon as possible, in the least number of years so that you pay less interest. If possible, acquire within 5 years.

There are different ways to install a solar system. One option is to install it independently from the electrical grid (also known as Off-the-grid or Stand-alone). In this case, the major cost is the battery bank. But the advantage is that you have electricity, even during a power outage, or blackout.

The second option is a system tied to the grid with Net-Metering. In this case the system is less expensive because you do not have to buy batteries. The disadvantage is that, during a power outage, you won't have electricity. But normally, if you generate more energy than you consume, you can sell it back to the Electric Power company. However, in Puerto Rico it is usually better to design your system so that it does not generate too much extra energy, but rather generates practically what you are going to use, or a little bit below that, because if you generate extra, you are only paid back a fraction of the price at which you buy it. Check on your area to see what the Net-metering regulations are.

A third option is a combination of the first two, it is known as a hybrid system. This system has a smaller number of batteries, just enough to operate for a few hours in case on a power outage or for days, depending on your needs. So, you never run out of electricity. The cost depends on several factors, how many kWh you use on average, for how many hours you want to have energy in case of an emergency (12 or 24 hours of refrigerator, 3 cloudy days, etc.).

Photovoltaic systems usually produce more energy when the outdoor temperature is cooler. In spite of this, solar energy can be used practically on the entire island of Puerto Rico, as long as the photovoltaic system is not too close to shades from trees or buildings.

Solar PV technology is becoming more and more efficient every day, and its cost has dropped considerably compared to only a few decades ago. But you have to see it as an investment and calculate the recovery time of this initial venture. After this time, which could be for example seven years, everything will be savings.

Now, I must emphasize that before thinking about installing a photovoltaic system in your home, you must understand something very important that you should do as the first step: **conservation.**

For a PV system to be cost-effective the appliances must be energy efficient, you must minimize (save) energy as much as possible. This means not installing a central air conditioning because the system would be too expensive, and the recovery time would then be too long for it to be cost-effective.

4.1.3 Stand-Alone Solar vs. Fuel generator

What is cheaper: an electric fuel generator or a solar photovoltaic system?

Correct answer: It is not the generator. From our experience after Hurricane Maria hit the island of Puerto Rico in 2017, which forced many to live without power for months, the basic solar system (as described below) costs about $1500 to $6000 (installed), the generator would cost at least $1000, plus $500 per month of fuel to operate for a <u>few hours a day</u>. For 3 months this adds up to $2500 That is, unless you plan to keep the generator off, the solar system turns out to be cheaper because its cost is recovered in less than 5 months.

In addition:

- The solar system can be <u>used all the time</u>, not only during a blackout. You can keep your fridge and other essential devices connected all the time, even if the electric company is working. So, the recovery of your investment is even faster.

- The sun is free. You will have free delivery to your home every day. ☺ This means no lines to buy diesel or gasoline are necessary.

- It does not generate smoke. This avoids discomfort with your neighbors, expenses from medicines or medical treatment due to respiratory problems and air pollution. It will also avoid the emission of greenhouse gases that worsen global warming and causes stronger hurricanes.

- It does not generate noise, which helps everyone to sleep better, and does not affect the natural cycles of the fauna.

Myths: Let's examine some of the myths.

Myth #1: The most common is to think that batteries are too expensive. The reality is that their price has gone down considerably in recent years. And they do not pay sales tax in many countries (including PR) if they are solar batteries. As of 2018, you can now get a bank of 24 Volt solar batteries for $600 or less.

Myth #2: Another myth is that, if there is a power outage, you run out of electricity too. This is not true for a battery system; it only applies to a grid-tied system.

Description of the Stand-alone Survival Solar System (S4)

This system described here is about having a "solar electric generator", especially for emergencies and after disasters. It is not to power air conditioners, microwaves, or hair blowers, but the basics: a small 10-15 cubic feet refrigerator (with Annual Energy Use of around 350 kWh/yr.), fans, cell phone chargers, several LED bulbs, radio and small TV.

The refrigerator would be on for 24 hours, the bulbs and others between 4-10 hrs. You could even connect a washing machine if you unplug the fridge while washing. It is presumed that the person has a gas stove.

This is a separate system from the grid and consists of 4 main components:

1. The **panels** of ~ 260W each

2. A **charge controller** - which regulates the current and feeds the batteries. Must be the MPPT (Maximum Power Point Tracking) type to maximize absorption of solar energy.

3. **Batteries** (Deep Cycle discharge, to have power when there is no sun: at night)

4. The **inverter** - which is what changes the DC current to AC current (the one used by most common appliances). It must be Pure-Sine-Wave type.

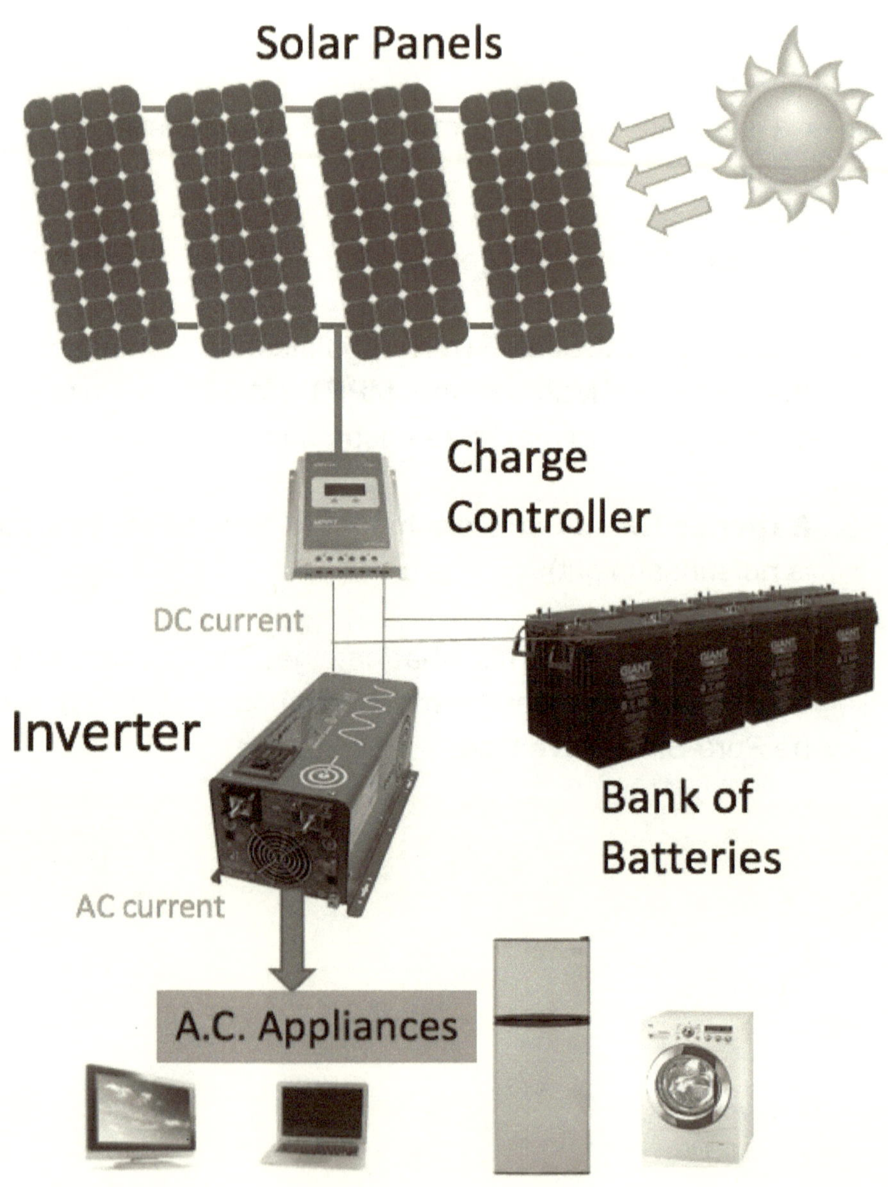

Solar Panels
Charge
Controller
DC current
Inverter
Bank of
Batteries
AC current
A.C. Appliances

How to calculate how many batteries, panels, etc., do you need?

You can download a calculator that I prepared at: http://ece.uprm.edu/~pol/s4/ . The file has two tabs, one in Spanish and one in English. Enter only your data in the YELLOW boxes. Do not change the others because they already have the equations to calculate how many panels and batteries you need, and what type of charge controller and inverter.

However, if you change them by mistake, it's ok, you can download the file again. The calculator also provides an estimate of the cost of materials and equipment as of 2018 (these materials are usually cheaper in the main USA). The two videos below give you more details.

> **Video 1:** Explain How to use the calculator:
> https://youtu.be/L93xp64uSYc
> **Video 2:** Explain how to connect them:
> https://youtu.be/TK46D6odWKk

Remember, the real cost of things should include the cost of operation, in this case the cost of fuel and motor oils. When we make the comparison, it is fair to include the COMPLETE cost; not only the initial cost but also add the cost of operation.

Above, the author installing solar panels for a photovoltaic system.

4.1.4 Energy from the Ocean

There are several types of energy from the ocean. For example: wave energy, which uses the movement of sea waves to generate electrical energy (high and low tides); and ocean-thermal energy (known as Ocean Thermal Energy Conversion, or OTEC), which uses the temperature difference between sea level and underwater to generate movement, and this movement generates electricity.

Energy from the ocean, is obtained in several ways.

Both of these alternatives are quite expensive and still have barrier which make them difficult to implement in the middle of the ocean. They have to be built with very expensive metals, to avoid or minimize rust, and they need lots of maintenance, an emergency backup plan in case of hurricane or storms, and also have other challenges that make it a not-so-viable alternative currently. Nevertheless, it is already being tested and used in some countries such as South Korea, Ireland, and the U.S.[31].

---

[31] https://blogs.ei.columbia.edu/2017/02/14/tapping-into-ocean-power/

5 ECOLOGICAL TRANSPORTATION

What means of transportation emits the most emissions: car, boat, train or plane? Which mode of transport is more efficient? Many countries are moving toward electric or hybrid cars and other modes of transportation that benefit air quality, save money, and have other benefits.

I invite you to do an experiment to think about the opportunities for improvement in transportation in your area. It consists of counting the number of passengers inside all cars you see during the mornings. You may notice that a lot of cars have only one or two people. This contributes heavily to increasing greenhouse gas emissions due to the use of fuel.

Who likes traffic jams?

Look at the image below, it's a comparison of the road space needed by the same number of people (60) if they use cars, public transport or bicycles. The photo was published in Germany.

Amount of space required to transport the same number of passengers (60) by car, bus or bicycle. Poster in city of Muenster Planning Office, August 2001. Credit: Pres-Office City of Münster, Germany

The huge advantages of using bicycles and public transportation, where available, are obvious; we lower gas emissions, less traffic jams, less pollution, and less noise.

Bicycles also improve your health and save a lot of money from gasoline and greenhouse gas emissions.

5.1 Types of Transport & their Environmental Impact

Transportation is responsible for many emissions of several greenhouse gases such as CO_2 and N_2O, among others, which constitute 14% of all emissions that trap heat in the atmosphere, which then eventually end up in our oceans and land.

In the next graph we can see the difference in the average emissions of total greenhouse gases due to transportation (which are called carbon dioxide equivalents, or CO_2e) for each type of transport means: land, air, ship, and rail according to the International Energy Agency (IEA) World Energy Outlook.

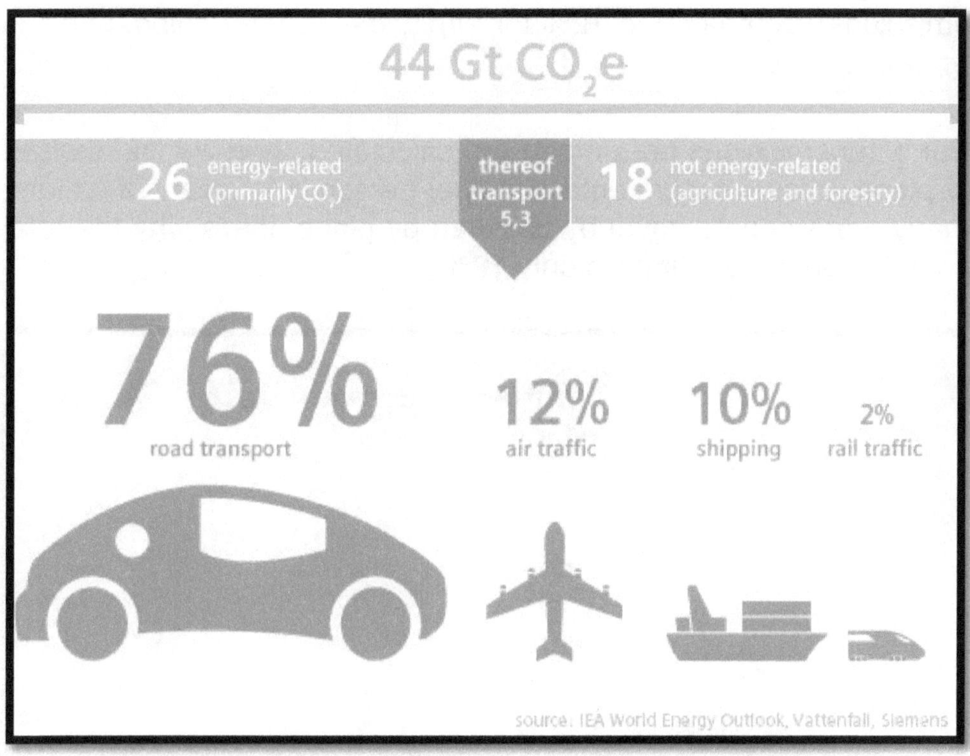

Comparison of transportation emissions from several means. Source: International Energy Agency (IEA) World Energy Outlook

Transportation produces greenhouse gas emissions that make up 14% of all those that heat our atmosphere. This 14% can be further decomposed as shown in this diagram above, where 76% (of the 14%) is due to trucks and cars.

Thus, the means of transportation that produces the most emissions is terrestrial, including trucks and cars, which are responsible for 76% of greenhouse gas emissions due to transport (not total global emissions), compared to 12% for airplanes, 10% for ships, and 2% for trains.

But if the emissions per person are calculated, then we find that an airplane produces more emissions per person than a car. Of course, many more people travel by car than by plane, that's why the total contribution for airplanes is only 12%.

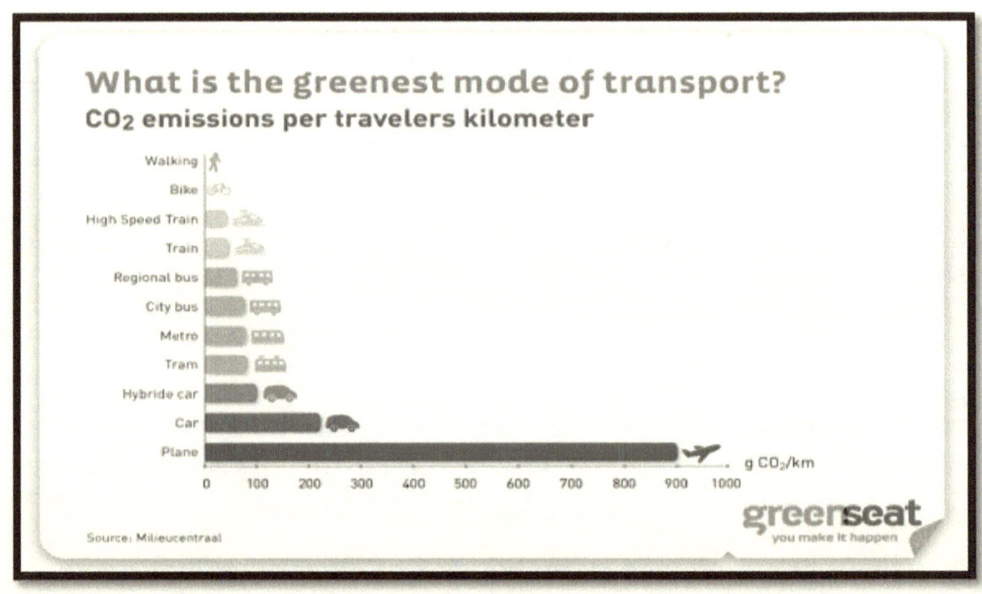

We also note that car emissions depend a lot on the car model and also on how many people share it.

Given that 95% of all means of transport use oil as fuel, it is not surprising that it is responsible for 14% of the total emissions of gases that heat our planet (www.ipcc.ch/report/ar5/wg3/).

The following chart of the UN World Bank (2004) shows the number of vehicles the population has as a function of per capita income.

In most countries, the richer the people are, the more cars they have. However, that does not necessarily improve the quality of life as we will see in another chapter. On the contrary, usually the quality of life increases when you can use mass transportation or bicycles daily.

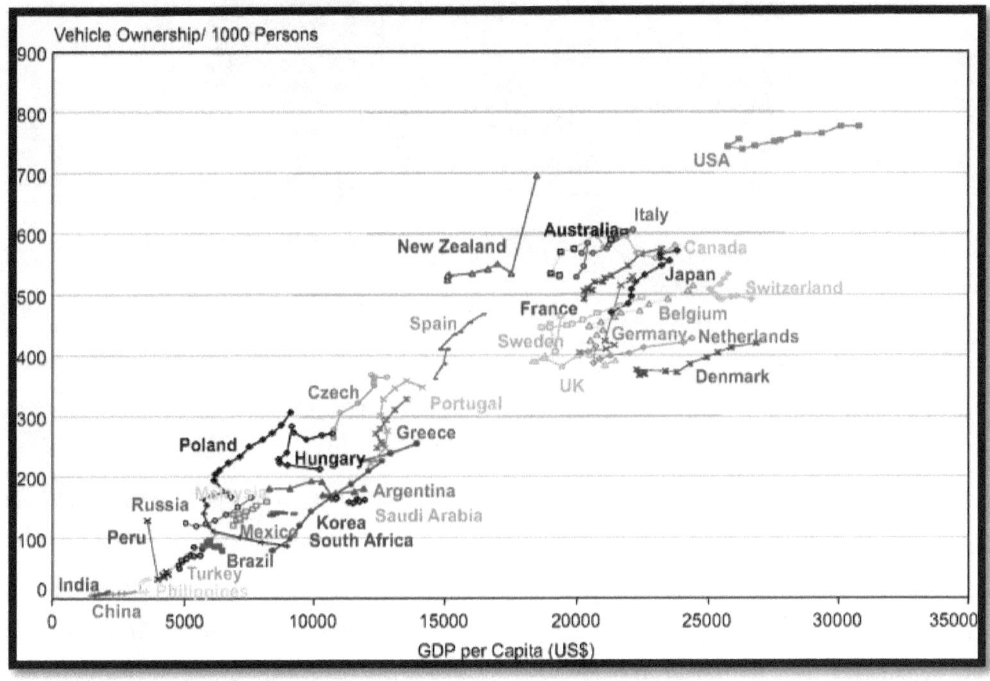

Number of vehicles the population has as a function of per capita income.[Source: UN World Bank, 2004]

The number of cars worldwide has increased considerably in recent decades. For instance, it went from 50 million vehicles in 1950 to 580 million in 1997. In 50 years, the population doubled – but the number of cars increased by a factor of more than 10!

In China, the number of cars rose three times in only 5 years!

After its economic reforms in 1978, opening to the global market in 1990, and joining the WTO, China economic growth rate increased considerably, and now its people want to live the 'American dream', have their TVs and their cars, instead of their traditional wheelbarrows or bicycles.

Trains are the most fuel-efficient means of transportation in terms of energy. The technology could be further improved in various ways that are currently being studied such as achieving less aerodynamic friction, breaking that regenerates energy, lighter trains materials, among many others.

During the 16th century, there were modern rail transport systems all over the world. They provided a very efficient means of mass transportation. Yet, with the advent of cars, owning a vehicle became widely accessible to the masses on the 20th century. This triggered the disappearance of the railroads in most countries to give space for building auto roads. In Puerto Rico there was a railway line along the coast of the island that unfortunately was replaced to make way for cars. on the link below there are more details on this map of the old railroads in Puerto Rico.

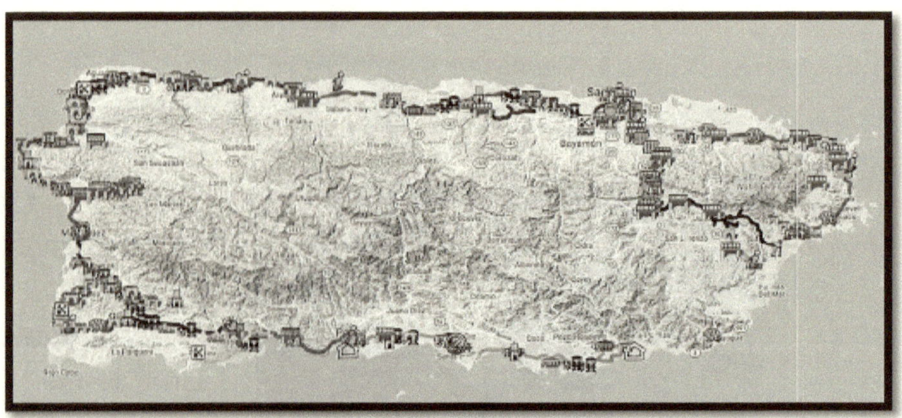

Map of Puerto Rico's old railroads
http://redescubriendoapuertorico.blogspot.com/p/blog-page.html

A great advantage of mass transportation, such as trains and buses, is that they provide time for people to relax, read or work while traveling. Another advantage is that it provides the elderly with a safer and more reliable means of transportation.

Ships transport 90% of the global merchandise. This is why they are important for trade. However, marine technology could improve considerably. The efficiency of the current fuel systems used by ships could increase by 40%.

Airplanes have already increased the efficiency with which they generate their energy by 70% compared to 40 years ago. And they are expected to continue improving. A concept that is already being planned is to replace communication cables by wireless communication to decrease the weight of the cables, which amount to about 15,000 lbs. (6,800 kg) in a typical passenger plane.

The lighter the airplane, the less fuel it uses. Other technologies are still under development to improve their efficiency, such as designing the shape of the aircraft body and the turbines.

However, something that is important to mention, is that aircrafts emit sulfur which, despite being a pollutant that causes acidification of the seas, and acid rain in the forests, it also lowers the global temperature.

In fact, just after the terrorist attacks of September 11, 2001, when all flights in the U.S. were canceled, the average global temperature rose by 3°F (1.7 C)! This is because the planes were not emitting sulfur, which is masking some of the effects of global warming!

But in addition to technology and engineering, policies that incentive the reduction of emissions are needed. In Paris 2015 (at the COP21 Climate Conference), measures to issue taxes for fuel and other regulatory instruments were discussed. Already 190 countries pledged to do their part to reduce their emissions of all kinds.

5.2 Advantages of the Bicycle

Another important means of transportation is the bicycle, as mentioned above. Every day there are more initiatives emerging all around the world that promote the use of the bike as a transportation and recreational means. Not only are they better for the planet and much cheaper, and they are also healthier for the user. But always remember to follow the traffic rules and use helmet and reflectors for your safety.

The human body is designed to exercise, walk, work the land, swim, run, and other activities.

But unfortunately, today most of us live a sedentary life, and this deteriorates our health. By using the bicycle, we save on gasoline, maintain better health, and take care of our environment (clean air, less noise and fewer gas emissions that cause global warming).

5.3 Ten Tricks to Save Gas

We already saw how to save money on water and electricity bills. Now you will learn how to save on gasoline. As we have mentioned, the use of fossil fuels such as gasoline produces emissions of greenhouse gases, that has changed our climate producing extreme events such as strong hurricanes, droughts, and floods. In fact, each gallon of gasoline our cars use produces 20 pounds of CO_2!

... What alternatives do we have?

We can save Gasoline!

MPG is a measure of fuel efficiency that stands for *miles per gallon*. In the next chart we see how MPG's minimum performance standard has improve, rising over the years in several countries.

As you can see in the chart, cars manufactured in the US cannot be sold in Japan because they do not meet their performance requirement. Europe and Japan require a minimum of 46 MPG, however, in the US the minimum is 26 MPG.

In fact, the state of California, in the U.S. has had to fight against the Environmental Protection Agency (EPA) to maintain the highest levels of performance in terms of miles per gallon, since the U.S. is one of the lowest in the world [32].

---

[32]www.extremetech.com/extreme/269202-will-california-go-to-the-mattresses-over-a-tougher-mpg-standard

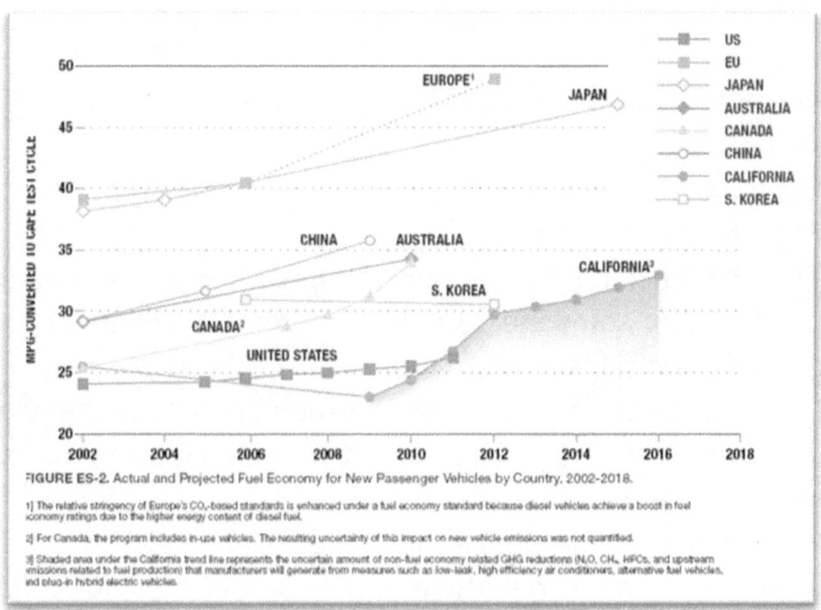

FIGURE ES-2. Actual and Projected Fuel Economy for New Passenger Vehicles by Country, 2002-2018.

Change over the years of cars minimum performance standard measured in *Miles Per Gallon* (MPG) in several countries and in California, USA.

And this is because even though the efficiency of the engines has improved, the cars are getting heavier, and require more fuel. According to the EPA, the MPG of new cars would be 24% higher in 2005 if the cars had maintained the weight and performance, they had in 1987.

10 Tips to Increase the gas performance of your car:

1. Accelerate as little as possible, that is, avoid the "heavy foot syndrome".
2. Combine trips in a way so that you always need to turn to the Right for the next trip.
3. Turn the ignition off while waiting more than 10 seconds. If you must wait for someone, turn your car off. It's a myth that turning it on will burn more fuel.
4. Do not use your car as storage: remember that the heavier the load, the more gas you use. So, if you need tools for safety, keep it to the bare necessities.
5. Keep your car tune-up, keep the tires filled to the appropriate level of air according to the manual specifications for your model.
6. Consider buying a hybrid or electric car. It is an initial investment that is paid in about 5-7 years.
7. Use the a/c or heater only when necessary, turning it off when the weather is fine, and turn it off when driving uphill; that will give more power to the engine, hence saving gas.
8. Whenever possible, park in the shade to prevent the fluids from evaporating from your car.
9. Avoid holes and speed reducers on the road, since they make you use more fuel.
10. Try to leave your home with enough time so you do not drive in a hurry, which will make you speed you up more, and therefore waste gasoline.

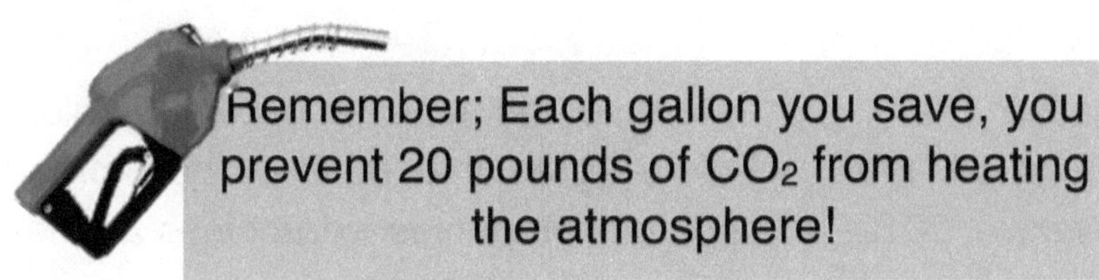

According to studies, the optimum speed at which the car saves more gasoline is 55 mph, as shown by this graph.

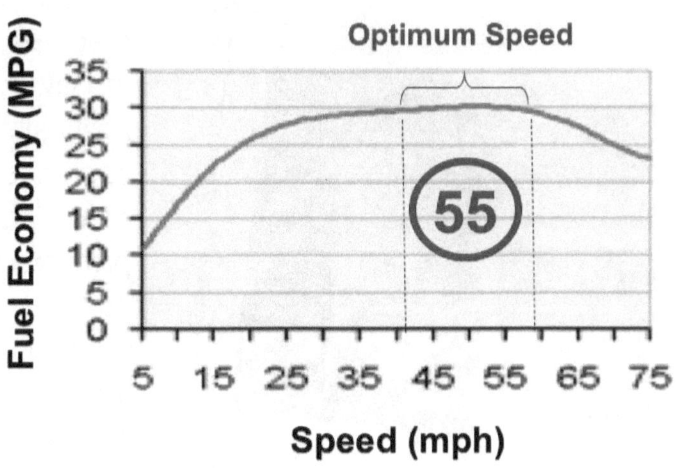

Of course, this only applies as long as the traffic laws allow it, not on a school zone! If you drive very slowly or very fast, the efficiency goes down, and it cost you more.

The so-called "Peak Oil" refers to the time of maximum global production of oil. Most scholars agree that peak oil has already passed (Nature, 2012) and that oil companies extract less and less oil every time from all their reserves. Oil reserves are running out. But, even if they weren't, we have learned the devastating consequences their burning has on our planet and climate.

In addition to this, reserves are mostly located in politically unstable countries. This has historically promoted many conflicts and even wars that could be avoided if renewable energy were encouraged.

Behind all this there are great interests from the oil and automotive industries. This is shown in the documentary "Who Killed the Electric Car?". The documentary shows the electric car of 1993, which yielded up to 125

MPG. It was able to accelerate from 0 to 60 mph in just 3.8 seconds and did not need oil changes.

Its engine was extremely clean and efficient, and produced zero greenhouse gas emissions. In spite all these benefits, it was destroyed in 1996 and the documentary examines the reasons behind this sad ending.

Look carefully before buying a new car, find out how much is its MPG. The car companies are often linked to the oil and gasoline, and are designing cars that spend more and more gas, instead of using technology of yesteryear, as is the case, for example, with the FIAT car.

Compare the MPG for the 1955 and 2011 models. Look how the MPG of the new design went down!

Car Model Year	Fuel Economy
FIAT 1955	55 - 60 MPG
FIAT 2011	27- 38 MPG

Could it be that engineers are not doing their job? Or they no longer know how to design well with high fuel performance? Or could it be that those who make the decisions above, the managers, the merchants, the industry leaders, decide to lower the efficiency at our expense and the planet's?

There are many technologies that have been researched and developed to make transportation more environmentally sound.

Examples:

- Use of other fuels such as gas, biofuels, and hydrogen.

- Vehicles that do not depend so much on these fuels.

- Compact 2-passenger vehicles; like the SmartCar with gasoline engine, but so small that uses little fuel. Almost all cars in Rome, Italy are like that.

- Electric cars such as the Tesla. Some models are still very expensive, although their prices are going down considerably. Some yield over 300 miles in between charges.

- Hybrid cars, which have two engines; one electric with a battery and one petrol (gasoline) motor, can regenerate energy every time you brake or decelerate. This allows for energy to be stored in a battery instead of being lost. In a regular gasoline car every time you brake, you lose the energy that was generated with the gasoline.

- Plug-in hybrids, which can be connected to charge their batteries. They also capture the energy every time you brake or decelerate.

Car Model	Fuel Economy
Hybrid Highlander	40 MPG
Prius	60 MPG
Hummer	3-12 MPG

In this table we can compare the fuel efficiency of two hybrid cars and the GM Hummer. The Hybrid Highlander yields up to 40 MPG, the Prius up to 60MPG, and Hummer between 3-12 MPG!

In my experience, hybrid cars are much cheaper than gasoline. I had a Hybrid Highlander for many years and the only thing I spent on repairs was a $3 fuse. I had it until we no longer had our daughters at home. I gave it in trade-in for a Toyota Prius and I have been with it for many years. Again, I have not had any problems with it in seven years so far. I have saved thousands of dollars in gasoline and with the credit offered by the government, and the price was similar to a car of comparable size. If I only use it for short local trips, a full tank yields for almost a month of usage.

Plug-in cars can last more than 200 miles between charges! The Chevy-Volt reaches 370 miles, which is more than enough for most people. In PR, the cars that can be charged by connecting them to the grid (Plug ins) are not yet common, but the government already began to plan charging stations in preparation for the introduction of these to the island.

The good news is that even if you use fossil fuel energy to charge an electric car, the total emissions will be less than that of a gasoline car as shown in the following map.

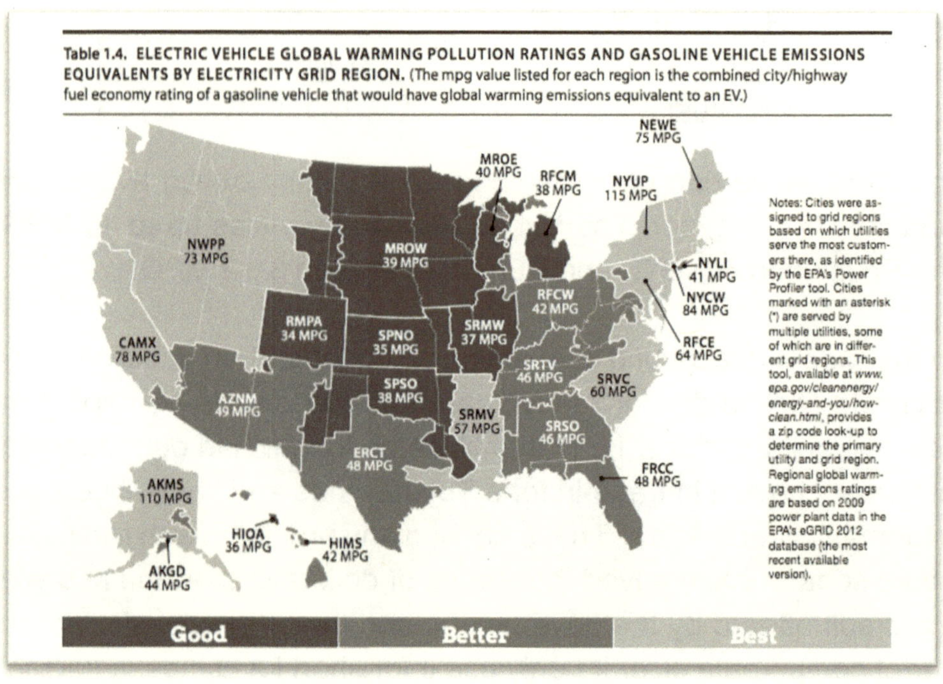

This map shows that the Impact on the planet depends on where an electric car is charged, since in each state the percentage of fossil/renewable used for energy generation is different. Of course, the ideal situation would be to charge it with renewable energy.

Some technologies, such as the hydrogen car, have yet to reduce their costs considerably in order to be economically viable.

But if you do not have money to buy a Prius and you want to help the planet (and your health) ... eat less meat or become vegetarian or vegan. (We'll talk about this in chapter 9).

5.6 Biofuels

Other solutions have been explored for many years. For instance, biofuels have the potential to replace part of the petroleum for transportation. Yet, some biofuels are not very efficient, as is the case of corn-based bioethanol, because it takes the same amount of energy to produce the fuel that provides that amount of energy, that is, a ratio of 1:1. Contrariwise, for the biofuel made from sugarcane the energy-producing ratio is 1:8. That is, it produces 8 times more energy than what was used to produce the fuel (sugar cane ethanol).

Biofuel is also produced from seaweed. Recent estimates from the IEA (International Energy Agency) indicate that the proportion of biofuels for transport would increase by around 10% in 2030[33].

---

[33] http://www.iea.org/tcep/transport/biofuels/
"Global Warming: Methane," U.S. EPA, 8 Mar. 2006.
World Business Council for Sustainable Development Mobility 2001 (2002), prepared by MIT and Charles River Associates Inc., Automotive News Data

Public transport and bicycles should be promoted whenever possible. This includes renting cars and bicycles on the street. For all of these measures to take place, we need government support to create the infrastructure that facilitates them.

In some countries the solution has been to increase the cost of fuels, or *fuel tax* to promote their savings. Consequently, people are motivated to carpool, or use public transportation. Unfortunately, the cheaper the gasoline is, the more people use it, because most people do not think about the environmental impact, but about their economy. It is a short-term vision that must be changed with education.

Some of the solutions that have worked in some countries are to increase the minimum MPG of cars, and offer incentives for energy-efficient cars, such as hybrids and electric cars.

In summary, the best policy varies according to the region:
- The level of economic development
- The nature of the economic activity
- The geography
- The population density
- The culture and education

Center:
www.autonews.com/apps/pbcs.dll/search?Category=DATACENTER01archive

All these factors have some influence on the effectivity and steadfastness for public policies that decide the amount of investment on transport and other ecological. In the meantime, you can apply some of the environmental measures presented here and save money, while also helping the planet.

6 E-WASTE

Millions of electronic devices are discarded every single day! Learn about the environmental and social impact from the manufacture and waste of electrical and electronic equipment and how to minimize it.

Today we depend much more than ever on the use of electronic equipment for communications, commerce, and countless other activities. We want to have the latest technology, and we change our equipment more and more frequently than ever before.

However, we must not overlook the fact that all this has an impact on our planet, our health, and our wallet. So, let's take a closer look at e-waste.

6.1 What is e-waste?

The term refers to waste generated when disposing unwanted
electrical and electronic equipment such as computers, cell phones,
refrigerators, washing machines, televisions, and many other
appliances. See image below.

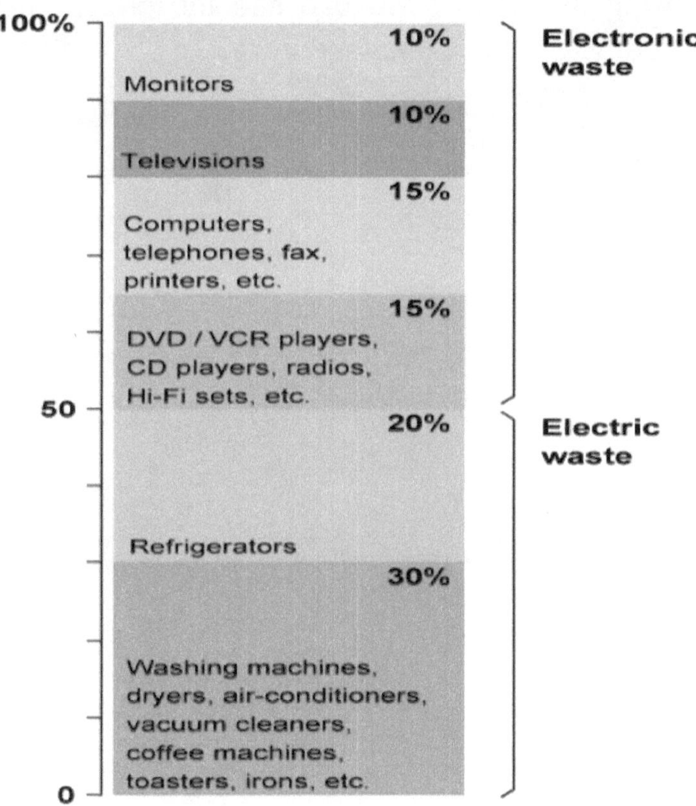

In just one-decade (between 1992-2002) sales of electronics
including computers increased by a factor of four (4)!

Additional categories include tubes of fluorescent lights, toys, safety equipment, among many others. Source: EMPA Swiss Federal Labs for Material Testing and Research (according to the European Union's (EU) Waste Electrical and Electronic Equipment (WEEE).

In the following two graphs we can see the growth in electronic device use for the case of China and India.

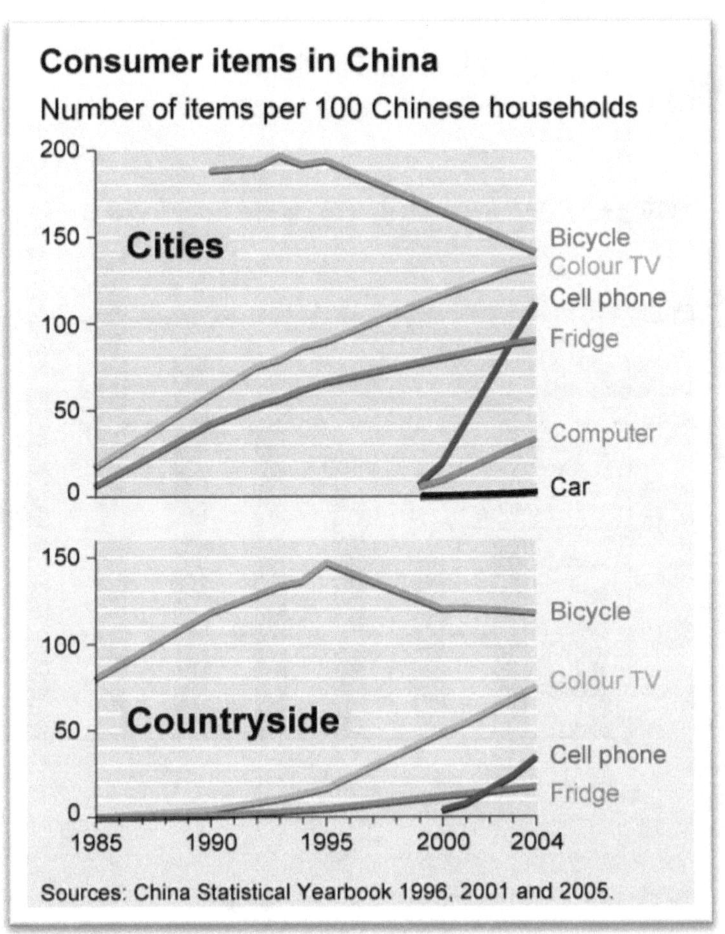

The fact that there are fewer and fewer bicycles, and more electrical equipment is distressing. By improving their economies, they have more access to buying more and more electronics. The amount of TV sets and cell phones acquired is growing exponentially.

Likewise, the acquisition of computers in India has increased exponentially in recent years.

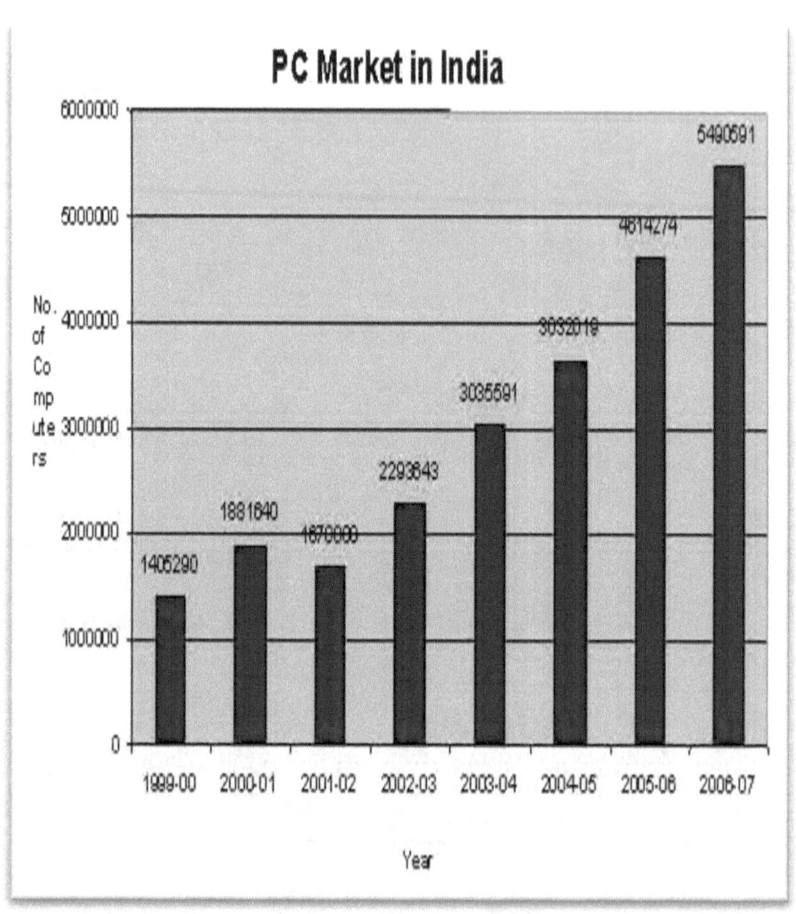

The next image presents the world map with the density of mobile phone use for the year 2011.

In many countries in Asia and Europe they use cell phones more than in the U.S. as shown on the map.

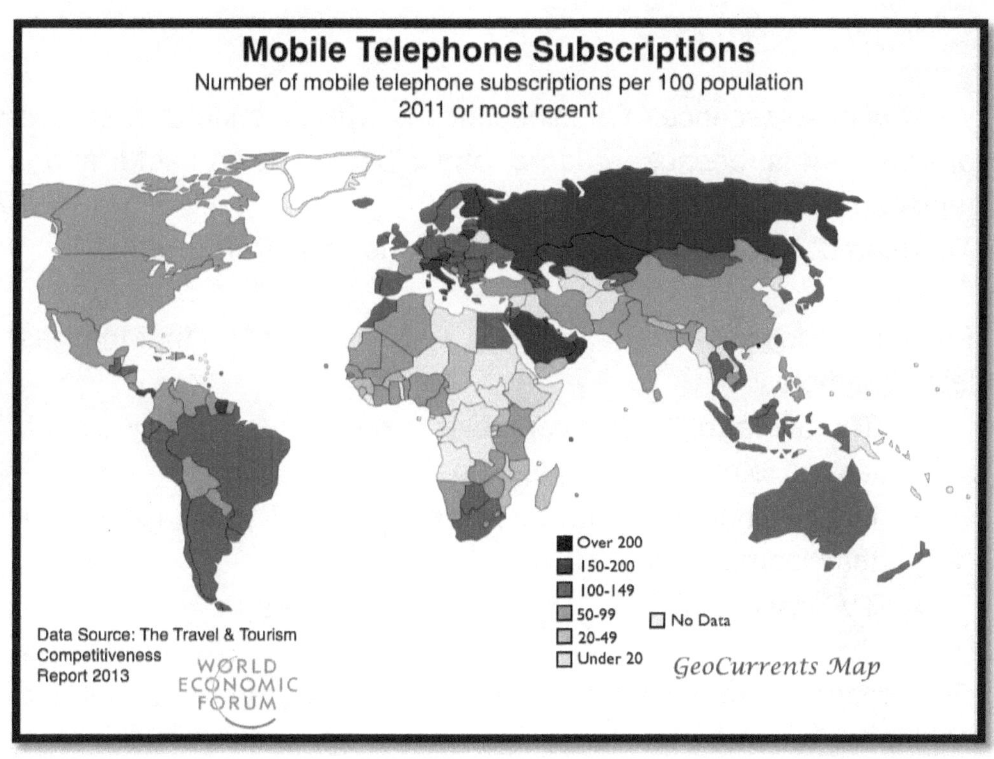

6.1.1 Electronic Waste Growth

Why does electronic waste grow so quickly?

- New appliances have infiltrated our daily lives, providing comfort, information, and communication.
- This is in addition to the fact that the appliances become obsolete more quickly. The useful life of the equipment is decreasing due to the fact that they become obsolete.

6.1.2 Obsolescence

What is obsolescence? Obsolescence is when the life of a product or object ends, because it is no longer perceived as useful and is replaced by another one.
There are 2 types of obsolescence: Planned and Perceived.

Planned obsolescence is when things are designed so that they last less. Examples.

- The average life of a computer is only 3 years! They used to last up to more than a decade.
- Mobile phones – current average life is 2 years (previously they lasted at least 10 years)
- TV – last about 4 to 13 years now, on average.

Remember when televisions lasted for decades? It is not that engineers are not able to design technology better now. It is all perfectly planned, so that people are forced to consume more.

The second type is the Perceived obsolescence:

- The model is designed so that another color, or shape, is in fashion, so that it is easy to identify if it is a new model.
- It is not done to improve functionality but to promote overconsumption, so that people want to buy a new item.

Both types of obsolescence respond to an economic model based on unlimited growth: which is NOT sustainable. So, we must ask ourselves if we really need to always have the latest model of electronic device or maybe it is a need created by marketing, utterly unnecessary, and that is costing us money and enriching others, and, on top of all this, it destructively impacting the planet and our health.

We have to replace consumerism, with the old tradition of keeping and fixing your stuff. The short documentary (~ 7 minutes) titled The Story of Electronics is available for free in several languages and several Internet sites, and briefly explains the concept of obsolescence.

6.2 What's inside the Electronics

Electronics contain a mixture of many types of materials, including plastics, glass, and metals.

Why is it difficult to dispose of electronics?

It's because of what's inside.
- Inseparable plastics (durable)
- Recyclable copper
- Glass, ceramics, difficult to separate
- Toxic metals: Lithium, Cd, Lead, Hg
- Coltan, & PCBs, PBDEs, TBBPA, TCE.

They often contain materials adhered to one another in such a way that it becomes practically impossible to separate. In addition, to reduce costs many cheap materials linked to diseases are used and pollute the environment.

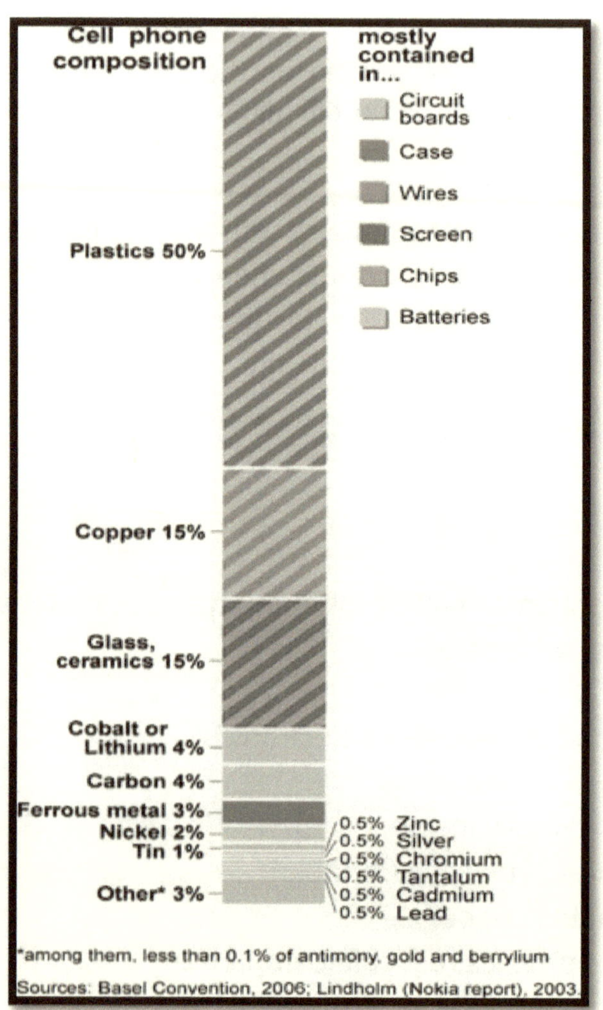

Cell phone composition
mostly contained in...
Circuit boards
Case
Wires
Screen
Chips
Batteries
Plastics 50%
Copper 15%
Glass, ceramics 15%
Cobalt or Lithium 4%
Carbon 4%
Ferrous metal 3%
Nickel 2%
Tin 1%
Other* 3%
0.5% Zinc
0.5% Silver
0.5% Chromium
0.5% Tantalum
0.5% Cadmium
0.5% Lead
*among them, less than 0.1% of antimony, gold and berrylium
Sources: Basel Convention, 2006; Lindholm (Nokia report), 2003.

Many of these materials are harmful to our health. Here is a partial list of some of the diseases linked to materials commonly used in electronic and electrical equipment. It is not surprising that diseases that once were rare are becoming more common. We are being exposed more and more to multiple toxins in our environment.

- Cancer
- Hormones disruptors
- Lung diseases
- Lead: colic, paralysis, atrophy of shoulder-waist muscles
- Chrome: produced when manufacturing plastics

- Allergic reactions, rashes, upset stomach, ulcers, irritation, and bleeding from the nose, respiratory problems in addition to affecting the immune system.
- Linked to several diseases such as Diabetes, Obesity, Birth Defects, Infertility, and others.
- Other symptoms: nausea, vomiting, rashes, headache, asthma, and the list goes on ...

When they reach nature, they kill microorganisms that we need for life, in rivers, soil, agricultural land, and so on, creating ecological chaos with detrimental repercussions on the environment and our health.

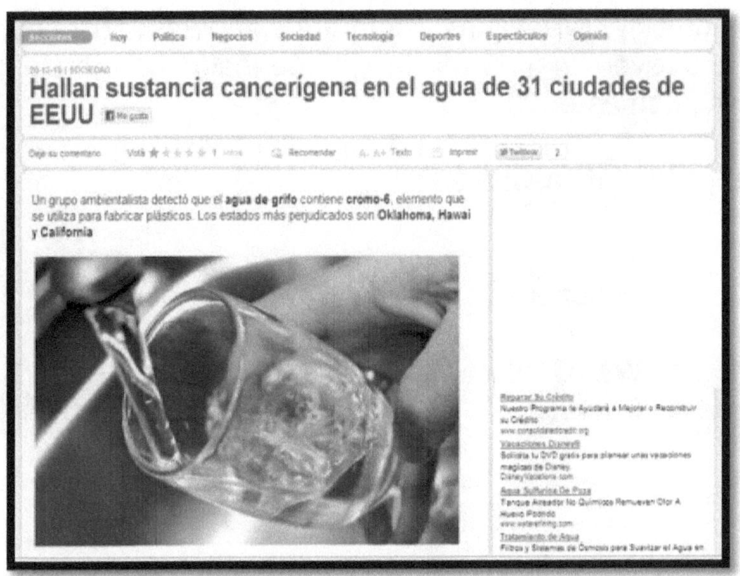

Some 2 million tons of electronic products became obsolete in 2005, of these, only 350 to 385 thousand tons are recycled. The other 1.5 to 1.8 million tons (80%) end their lives in landfills - according to EPA.

These toxins enter the soil and with the rain they leak into our water reserves. The Aqueduct and Sewer Authorities (in many countries, including Puerto Rico) are not capable of filtering heavy metals. Neither can regular commercial water filters such as Brita or Püre. More expensive osmosis or ceramic filters are needed. Bottled water is not immune to these toxins either.

6.4 Social Impacts: Extraction of Materials

Let's examine some examples of the social impacts of continuing to manufacture more and more electronics and dispose of them more and more quickly. We will see among its impacts: pollution, health, poverty and even war conflicts (in the case of metals used in electronics such as gold).

Social impacts of e-waste are:

- Pollution
- Health
- War Conflicts
- Poverty

In the latter case, for example, it is known that gold mines finance civil wars in some African countries. And they produce mercury as a byproduct, which is highly toxic to humans.

To make electronics you need to extract many materials

- The process of extracting gold and copper includes acid baths and requires physical manipulation.

- Mercury is produced during gold extraction and evaporates into the environment during the process.

- Plastic, which contains brominated flame retardants (BFR), emits BFR and toxic gases into the environment when recycled.

The waste reaches the sewage system or nearby land, which contributes to the contamination of water and soil.

The majority of people working in this recycling sector are poor with very low levels of education and with very little awareness of the risks of toxic substances from electronic waste. There are a considerable number of women and children who engage in these activities and are more vulnerable to the dangers of this type of waste. Many of these people have no alternative but to accept these deplorable working conditions.

Think about this before accepting free cell phones: someone pays with their health, and we pay all with the pollution of our environment.

6.5 Social and Environmental Impacts: Recycling

During recycling, it is necessary to break and segregate dangerous components, and sometimes even burn PVC wires to extract copper. They also have to burn and melt lead and components containing mercury.

This provides work that has promoted the abandonment of agriculture for mining, in occasions have produced famines in these countries.

Many times, school children are the ones working and exposing themselves to these toxins. And these children are more vulnerable to the biological effects of these toxins because their bodies are still developing.

Working conditions in mines are another social impact. They are deplorable and very risky, as you might recall from many incidents of miners trapped in mines collapse.

In 2010, some miners were rescued after remaining months underground (69 days in the incident in Chile)[34], but thousands perish annually in many countries. And we could claim that they die unnecessarily, since most metals can be recycled indefinitely.

---

[34] https://nypost.com/2014/10/11/how-the-chilean-miners-men-survived-for-69-days-beneath-the-earths-surface/

If we used gold and other metals for electronics instead of jewelry, these miners could look for another less dangerous job.

The effects of mining go beyond accidents in mines. In this graph we see the emissions to both the soils and water bodies that occur in Australia due to the mining of metals such as nickel, gold, copper, iron, and others. This is similar in all countries where mines are present.

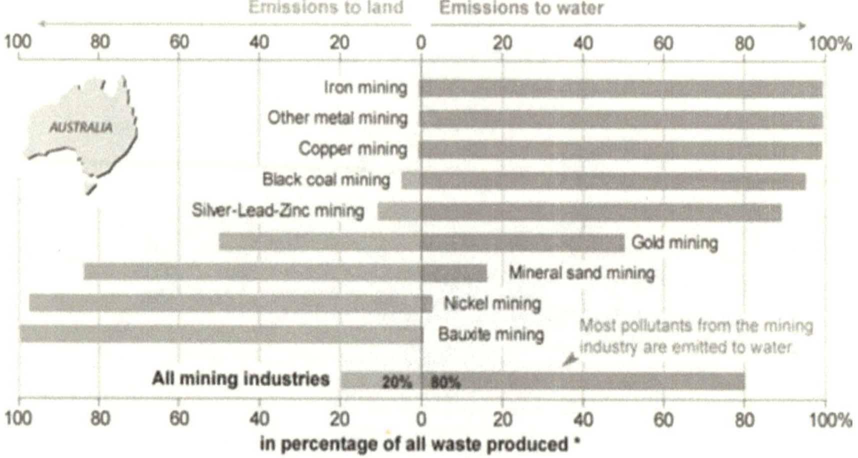

* Emissions to air are not taken into account (they are not considered as 'waste' per se).
Source: Australian National Pollutant Inventory, 2006 (figures for 2004).

Another effect of not designing things so that they can be easily recycled is that many are disguised as "donations" to poor countries where there are no laws that regulate these entries, and in reality they are useless. They have become an easy, yet illegal, way to dispose the trash from industrialized countries to developing countries.

In those cases, they usually end up burning the e-waste, and that makes the situation even worse because when incinerated they cause chemical reactions that create much worse toxins like dioxins.

6.6 Ecologic Solutions

As ecological solutions to this problem, three are presented here:

1.   Stricter laws that promote recycling and proper disposal of these wastes.

2.   "Cradle to Cradle" (C2C) Design, that is, design that facilitates the reuse of the materials of which the equipment is composed for a new equipment. Currently there are mostly designed as "Cradle to the Grave", that is, designed thinking that it cannot be used again.

3. Establish more equipment return programs to the company that manufactures them for recycling

We would be imitating a mango tree, for example. Where after the harvest season, it seems that many mangos are wasted on the soil, but in reality, they rot and serve as fertilizer to the tree for next year's harvest.

In many respects we must imitate Nature.

6.7 Take-back Appliance Programs

Some companies have programs that accept free return of their devices after they useful life. Below we see some examples.

However, sometimes the same company that offers this service in a country does not offer it in others, perhaps because the law does not require it.

- Cell Phones: AT&T
- TV: Samsung, LG, Sony PC: *Apple accepts them only in Japan and Taiwan

Prevention is designing so that the raw material can be reused once the life cycle of an appliance ends. It's cheaper in the long run if we consider the cost of cleaning the air / water from the pollution of e-waste and the cost of health services.

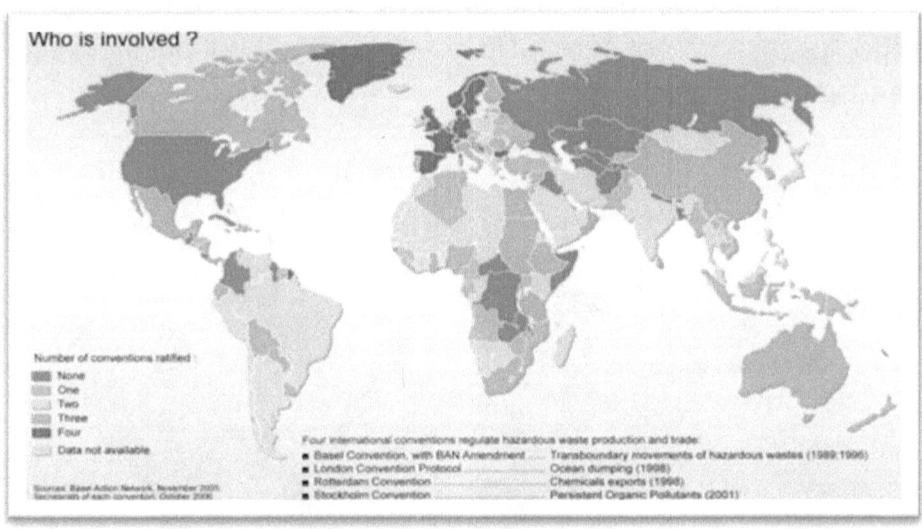

This map shows the countries that do have laws to regulate the disposal of toxic products (shown in dark green)[35]. The colors

---

[35] Based Action Network, 2005, 2006

indicate how many regulations they have, up to a maximum of four (4) international conventions that protect the ocean, export of chemicals, hazardous waste, and persistent organic pollutants.

Red countries such as the U.S., Russia, and Colombia do not have any of these regulations for the exchange and production of hazardous waste. Citizens pay with their health.

6.8 Green Electronics

Can human beings generate creative ideas on how to design electronics that are not harmful to health, and without polluting lakes, air and soil? Of course!

Recyclable laptop designed by a group of students from Stanford University and the University of Aalto in Finland in 2011.

For example, in 2011 a group of students from Stanford University and the University of Aalto in Finland designed a recyclable laptop in just 9 months! [36] See photo above.

It could be disassembled:

- In 10 steps
- Without tools
- In less than 2 minutes

Why don't industries implement this or similar products? Is it cheaper to do it in another way? Lack of laws? Maybe customers don't demand it?

Probably, a combination of several factors. But solutions will start to appear if people become aware and demand regulations that already exist in other countries.

---

[36] GreenBiz, "Recyclable Laptop Designed for Disassembly"
https://www.greenbiz.com/blog/2011/02/01/recyclable-laptop-designed-disassembly 2011

7 PERSONAL CARE PRODUCTS

Did you know that some makeup and other beauty and cleaning products contain ingredients that have been linked to cancer, diabetes, and other serious diseases?

Did you know that mineral oil comes from **Petroleum?** Did you know that women do not have to use **sanitary napkins ever?**

It is important that you are informed of these things so that you make wise, informed decisions when buying, and protect the health of your family and yours. At the same time, you will be protecting our environment (rivers, soils, beaches) from toxic and helping to prevent further global warming!

You can save money and gain health by following the tips that appear here. I invite you to watch the video: **The History of Cosmetics**, available on the Internet. It's about 7 minutes long, and it will change your life. It does not only speak of cosmetics but of many products that we use every day.

In this chapter you will learn how to identify eco-friendly personal hygiene products including cosmetic products and identify cleaning and household products free of contaminants.

You will also learn a recipe for homemade beauty lotion; economical and easy to make with natural ingredients, and many homemade recipes for cleaning products.

7.1 The Most Important Tip: Read the List of Ingredients!

Read the Ingredients, NOT the front of the label!

The most important advice I can give you in this chapter is to read the back of the labels, the list of ingredients and learn to understand it. Legally, manufacturers can put practically anything they want on the front of the label: words like "Natural", "ecological" don't mean anything certain. However, the law regulates the list of ingredients.

A Challenge for you:
Can you pronounce the ingredients in your cosmetics? If the answer is no, it is possible that they are petrochemical based. A vast majority of these ingredients have not been tested for toxicity.

Download the Environmental Working Group (EWG) application called *SkinDeep* on your mobile phone, it will help you choose healthy products. It's free! They welcome donations, which given their work, are very much well-deserved. You can also visit their website http://www.ewg.org/skindeep/app/

Below is a list of 14 ingredients that you should always try to AVOID:

DEA, MEA , TEA	Mineral Oil
Phthalates,	(polietilenglicol)
FD&C Colors	Propilenglicol
Fragrance	Sodium Lauryl
Imidazolidinylurea,	Sulfate (SLS) and
DMDM hydantoin	Sodium Sulfate
Quaternium – 15	Laureth (SLS)
Parabens	Triclosan
PEG	Talc, Vaseline

For example, mineral oil comes from petroleum, but it is a lot cheaper than using vegetable oils. Vegetable oils and lanolin are a lot more similar at the molecular level to the natural oils on your skin and therefore, are better for you, more efficient and not harmful. But to increase their profits, many companies opt for mineral oil.

In the SkinDeep database, you can enter the name of the product you use or one of its ingredients and it will display a number between zero (0) and ten (10), where the higher the number, the greater the risk that it might be toxic to your health. Each number has a corresponding color from green (for low numbers), yellow (for moderate) to red (for high numbers), indicating higher risk.

You will find that often times products of the same company have good and bad ratings, so it's not as simple as choosing a brand and sticking to it.

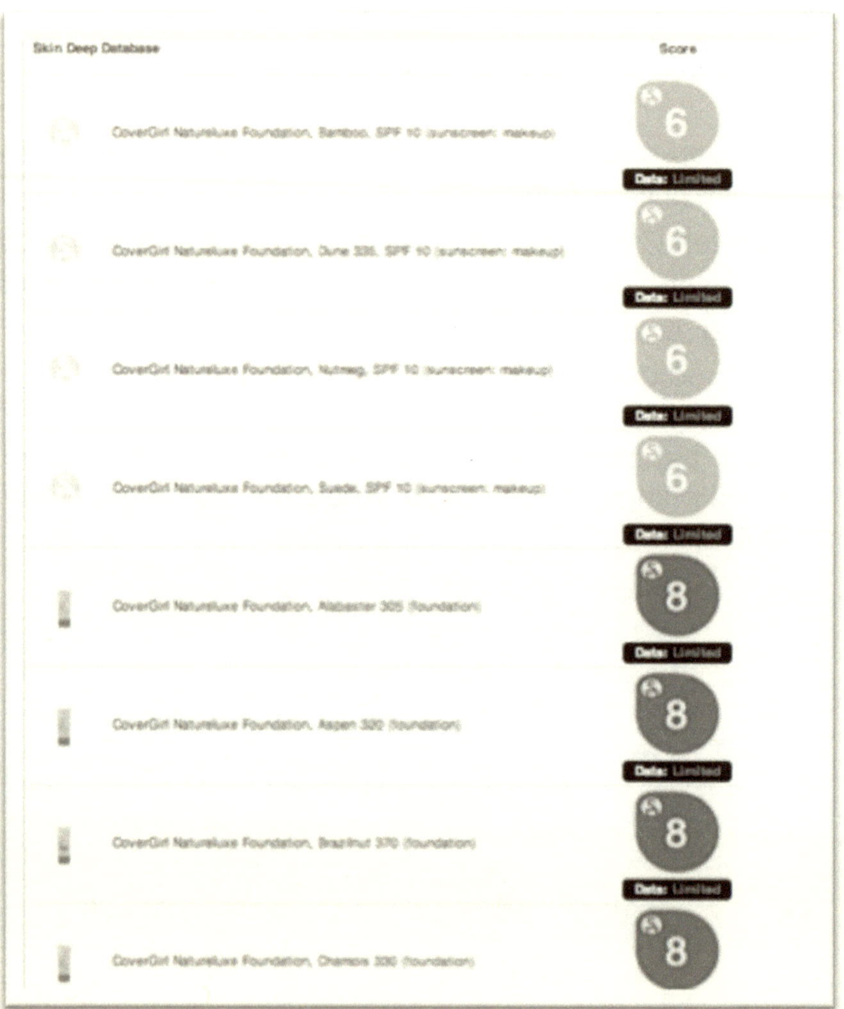

EWG Skin Deep, is a free website and App for your cell phone. Avoid products that appear in red.

Another example is the word "fragrance", which refers to petrochemicals that are aromatic. However, due to manufacturers' patent laws, the companies are exempt from disclosing their components. These petrochemicals are much cheaper than natural essences, but over 90% have not been tested for toxicity or how they interact amongst each other. That is why it is preferable instead to use natural perfumes or aromas derived from essential oils. These are extracted from biological sources such as lavender flowers, vanilla, or sandalwood.

Other products that we must avoid are all those who claim to be *anti-bacterial*. These contain *triclosan*. According to numerous studies, these products do more harm than good and are completely unnecessary [37] . Triclosan has been linked to cancer, bone deformation, weakness, and atrophied muscles.

In fact, even the FDA advises that it should not be used because it creates resistance in bacteria [38]. So, save your money and clean your hands with regular soap and water. (See section 7.3).

---

[37] WHO, Geneva, WHO Guidelines on Hand Hygiene in Health Care: First Global Patient Safety Challenge Clean Care Is Safer Care, 2009.
https://www.ncbi.nlm.nih.gov/books/NBK144041/
[38] https://www.ewg.org/enviroblog/2016/09/toxic-triclosan-banned-soap-lingers-consumer-products#.WzAlRxlzqrl

Did you know that some baby shampoos, and some sunscreens and suntan lotions have ingredients that cause cancer? Fortunately, in 2014 after a petition to the company Johnson & Johnson, with thousands of signatures, the company decided to change its baby shampoo formula to eliminate 2 ingredients that have been linked to cancer [39]. But even today there are still hundreds of hygiene and beauty products such as lipsticks, lotions, sunscreen, shaving creams, and others that contain ingredients linked to cancer and other disease.

You can educate yourself about it: look at the list on this the EWG Skin Deep Database where you can check how safe for your health are the products you currently use.

7.2.1 Sanitary Napkins

One product that women use a lot of our lives are sanitary napkins and tampons. They contribute to creating waste and are a

---

[39] https://cvskinlabs.com/after-years-of-pressure-jj-removes-cancer-causing-chemicals-from-baby-bath-products/

considerable expense in a woman's life, representing an average of seventy dollars ($ 70) each year!

In addition, they contain chloride and other chemicals that can cause allergies and infections. There is a product that replaces feminine towels and can be used for life. It has many advantages besides obviously reducing waste and cost. It is much more comfortable and effective, and it is easy to learn how to use it.

They come in various materials such as silicone or latex. It has been in the market for over 75 years; however, it is not yet well known in some parts of the world. It costs approximately half of what you spend in only one year on feminine towels.

How is it used? You can use them up to 12 hours in a row, depending on your flow; on the beach, when you sleep, you do not even feel them! It's super comfortable. It can be washed with only soap and water (for example, while you shower). In between periods you can wash it and then leave it for a few hours, in a combination of white vinegar or hydrogen peroxide mixed in equal parts with warm water. It takes a few days to get used to using it.

Thus, it's a great idea to invests in a silicone or natural latex cup, such as the DivaCup or the LadyCup. There are two sizes, for women who have given birth (or older than 26 years) and for those who have not. After using size 2, it can be reused for the rest of your life, saving you a lot of money and is better for your health and the environment. So, forget about sanitary napkins and tampons.

7.2.2 Beauty Salon Products

Be careful with other products that are used in beauty salons such as products to straighten your hair. Again, many contain highly toxic ingredients, so is preferable to check in the database whether they harm your health and the planet's. Some beauty salons obtain the Green Salon Certification, which indicates that they have completed a training on how to use eco-friendly, safe products.

7.2.3 Sunscreens

Did you know that some sunscreens contain ingredients that cause cancer? Isn't it ironic? don't you think? Avoid those that contain **oxybenzone;** is a synthetic estrogen that mimics our hormones and has been linked to cancer. Also avoid **retinol because** it makes your skin more sensitive to sun exposure.

Chemical	EWG hazard score	FDA 2019 proposed status	Skin penetration	Hormone disruption	Skin allergy	Other concerns
UV filters with higher toxicity concerns						
Oxybenzone[1]	8	Insufficient data and concern for absorption through skin and hormone disruption	Detected in nearly every American; found in mothers' milk; 1% to 9% skin penetration in lab studies	Weak estrogen, moderate anti-androgen; associated with altered birth weight in human studies	Relatively high rates of skin allergy	N/A
Octinoxate [2] (Octyl methoxycinnamate)	6	Insufficient data to determine safety – significant	Found in mothers' milk; less than 1% skin penetration in human and laboratory studies	Hormone-like activity; reproductive system, thyroid and behavioral alterations in animal studies	Moderate rates of skin allergy	N/A
UV filters with moderate toxicity concerns						
Homosalate [3]	4	Insufficient data to determine safety – significant data gaps	Found in mothers' milk; skin penetration less than 1% in human and laboratory studies	Disrupts estrogen, androgen and progesterone	N/A	Toxic breakdown products
Octisalate[4]	4	Insufficient data to determine safety – significant data gaps	Skin penetration in lab studies	N/A	Rarely reported skin allergy	N/A
Octocrylene [5]	3	Insufficient data to determine safety – significant data gaps	Found in mothers' milk; skin penetration in lab studies	N/A	Relatively high rates of skin allergy	N/A
UV filters with lower toxicity concerns						
Titanium dioxide[6]	2 (topical use), 6 (powder or spray)	Generally recognized as safe and effective	No finding of skin penetration	No evidence of hormone disruption	None	Inhalation concerns
Zinc oxide[7]	2 (topical use), 4 (powder or spray)	Generally recognized as safe and effective	Less than 0.01% skin penetration in human volunteers	No evidence of hormone disruption	None	Inhalation concerns
Avobenzone[8]	2	Insufficient data	Very limited skin penetration	No evidence of hormone disruption	Breakdown product causes relatively high rates of skin allergy	Unstable in sunshine, must be mixed with stabilizers
Mexoryl SX[9]	2	Insufficient data	Less than 0.16% skin penetration in human volunteers	No evidence of hormone disruption	Skin allergy is rare	N/A

References

[1] Janjua 2004, Janjua 2008, Sarveiya 2004, Gonzalez 2006, Rodriguez 2006, Krause 2012, Ghazipura 2017

[2] Krause 2012, Sarveiya 2004, Rodriguez 2006, Klinubol 2008

[3] Krause 2012, Sarveiya 2004, Rodriguez 2006, Klinubol 2008

[4] Krause 2012, Sarveiya 2004, SCCNFP 2006

[5] Walters 1997, Shaw 2006, Singh 2007

[6] Krause 2012, Bryden 2006, Hayden 2005

[7] Gamer 2006, Nohynek 2007, Wu 2009, Sadrieh 2010, Takeda 2009, Shimizu 2009, Park 2009, IARC 2006b

[8] Gulson 2012, Sayes 2007, Nohynek 2007, SCCS 2012

[8] Klinubol 2008, Bryden 2006, Hayden 2005, Montenegro 2008, Nash 2014

[9] Benech-Kieffer 2003, Fourtanier 2008

* Environmental Working Group-https://www.ewg.org/sunscreen/report/the-trouble-with-sunscreen-chemicals/

Sunscreens guide adapted from the *Environmental Working Group*

Every time you buy a product remember to check the list of ingredients. It is good to give your monetary support to initiatives such as EWG (ewg.org) as they do the work that government agencies should do, but unfortunately, due to many reasons, they do not.

7.2.4 Beauty Lotions

It is important to learn about the ingredients of everything you buy, including beauty and personal hygiene products. Remember, for example, that mineral oil comes from petroleum. Read the labels, not just the front part.

For beauty products, there are some very expensive brands that nevertheless use mineral oil as base. Many people pay dearly for this, for example, almost all Victoria's Secret creams are based on mineral oil. In addition, most products include chemicals used as fragrances and dyes (like Red # 5). Natural perfumes (such as essential oils extracted from flowers) are much more expensive and would decrease their profit margins.

If it says "FRAGANCE", it refers to petrochemicals; make sure that perfumed scents come from natural sources such as lavender, vanilla (not imitation), gardenias, etc.

Another way to save money is by making your products at home. Try this DIY recipe for skin lotion. It is very effective, economical, and easy to do. I have used it for more than 20 years.

It contains only 4 natural ingredients, and even if you buy all the ingredients organic, it is much cheaper than the products sold on beauty shelves in stores. It only contains equal parts of peanut oil and olive oil, a few drops of lanolin and rose water. Rose water is mixed when you apply, or you can mix all and keep for 1 week so that it doesn't become rancid. But be careful if you buy the very cheap rose water, you are probably buying artificial chemicals and that is not the same for your skin. Remember to read the ingredients on the back of the label. It takes about 12 rose petals to make an ounce of rose water. This mix is also available ready to be used on the internet at baar.com.

7.3 The Fallacy of Antibacterial Products

Would it be logical to eliminate all people because a few of them are criminals? Absurd! is it not? Something similar is done by chemical detergents such as chlorine, chemical disinfectants, and others by indiscriminately eliminating both beneficial and harmful bacteria. *Chlorine-based bleach, for example, is like a crazy cop who kills 99% of the population just because there are 1% criminals.* **It would be like killing all people in your town or country, just because a minority has a bad reputation.**

Bacteria have a bad reputation too. Yet, without bacteria, there would be no chocolate, yogurt, cheese, organic agriculture or even, healthy humans. Ecological cleaners are like an *intelligent policeman* who only catches the criminals, leaving free all the beneficial and necessary bacteria for good health.

According to the **World Health Organization (WHO)**, antibacterial products do more harm than good because they **promote the resistance of bacteria to antibiotics.** Therefore, you should avoid everything that contains Triclosan and <u>avoid all cleaning products that eliminate 99% of the bacteria</u>, as they damage your health and your environment (fauna, flora, bodies of water).

7.4 Cleaning Products

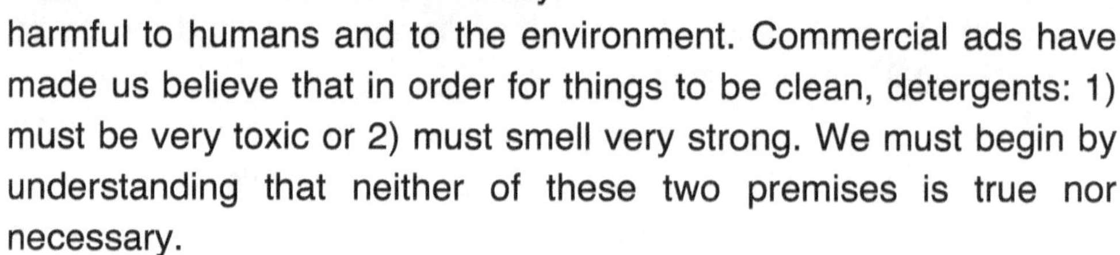

As in the case of hygiene products, many cleaning products contain toxins that are extremely harmful to humans and to the environment. Commercial ads have made us believe that in order for things to be clean, detergents: 1) must be very toxic or 2) must smell very strong. We must begin by understanding that neither of these two premises is true nor necessary.

Which products harm our health and poison the planet?

Almost all detergents that smell very strong, even if it is a pleasant smell like the artificial scent of flowers, are harmful. Avoid chlorine, as it has been linked to cancer in laboratory animals[40]. Many also cause asthma, allergies, and eyes or skin irritation. Think of all the extra expense this implies in terms of medical treatment and medications.

A better alternative for cleaning is to use white vinegar since it only kills bacteria that cause bad odor and harmful bacteria. Tea Tree oil, which comes from an Australian tree common now in Puerto Rico, Florida, and other regions, has anti-fungal, anti-viral, and antibacterial properties. However, they are also selective, so they do not kill all the bacteria, such as those necessary for a healthy life.

---

[40] Colorectal cancers and chlorinated water, World J Gastrointest Oncol. 2016

Here is a list of some of the ingredients that are used in the manufacture of ecological cleaning products. Except for borax and some of the essential oils, most are even edible. This provides an added advantage: it's safer for homes with small children.

- White vinegar
- Baking soda
- Common salt
- Lime or lemon juice
- Essential oils

Furthermore, in many occasions you can use the cleaning product to heal wounds and acne, something that cannot be done with toxic products. This makes them super convenient.

Save money and help the environment by avoiding antibacterial products (containing Triclosan) and using the simple recipes provided here for cleaning products which are as effective or more effective and do not contain harmful chemicals that cause asthma, allergies, irritable skin, and other health conditions and diseases. For most cleaning surfaces, like counters or floor, a mixture of white vinegar and water should suffice.

7.5.1 Essential oils

Some essential oils should not be consumed, as is the case of Tea tree oil. Many of these oils have anti-germ, anti-fungal, and anti-viral properties. This triple advantage is not possible with alcohol or Triclosan.

- Lavender
- Rosemary
- Melaleuca (tea tree)
- Mint
- Cloves
- Lemongrass
- Pine tree
- Eucalyptus
- Oregano
- Thyme

The important thing about essential oils is to use them well diluted in a base. The base can either be an oil such as almond or olive, or a liquid such as alcohol, witch hazel or simply water, depending on the application.

7.6 Cleaning Recipes

Anti-fungal and anti-germ spray
¼ tsp. lavender oil
¼ tsp. tea tree oil
2 cups of white vinegar
(squeeze the juice of a lemon - optional)

Mix in spray bottle. This simple product removes mold from bathroom curtains, kills germs, smells good, leaves everything clean and also removes grease stains. White vinegar penetrates porous surfaces and kills the root of the fungus, something chlorine cannot do.

Chlorine does not remove Fungus
That's why chlorine makes fungus stronger! Chlorine removes the outside part of the fungus, but in a few days, it grows stronger because chorine cannot penetrate porous surfaces. This wastes your money by forcing you to reapply very often. This is a common case when you clean your shower curtain. Use the recipe above instead, and you won't have to reapply every week, just probably once a year.

If we really want to have our hands and those of our loved ones clean, using soap and water is enough. If you work in a hospital, the WHO recommends using 70% alcohol to wash your hands, not anti-bacterial.

Mopping Cleaning solution

1 cup of vinegar
1 bucket of cold or warm water
5-10 drops of lavender or pine essential oil (optional)

Wood furniture cleaning solution

½ cup of olive or coconut oil (or bees wax)
¼ cup of lemon juice
 Mix in glass jar and apply with cloth to the furniture for a shine that nourishes the wood.

Hand Dishwashing liquid

1-ounce castile liquid soap
2 cups of water
1 tsp. of vegetable glycerin

Detergent for Dishwasher machines

A few drops of liquid dishwasher soap
1-2 Tbs. Washing soda or baking soda
½ Tbs. table Salt

¼ cup citric acid
1½ cup borax (powder or crystal, available at hardware stores and supermarkets)
15 drops of your favorite essential oil (optional)

This mixture of oils was used during the Bubonic Plague in Europe (1340-1400) to steal the possessions from the victims' corpses without being contaminated. According to several sources the ingredients are:

- 40 drops of clove essential oil
- 35 drops of lemon essential oil
- 20 drops of cinnamon essential oil
- 15 drops of eucalyptus essential oil
- 10 drops of rosemary essential oil

One drop of this mixture can be diluted for every ounce of base (water, vinegar or oil, for example). This mixture is super strong and should only be used in extreme cases to disinfect strong viruses or bacteria.

This simple recipe is very easy to prepare. Mixing equal parts of water and white vinegar will suffice, although you can add a few drops of your favorite essential oil. In the case of mirrors with calcium deposit stains, add a teaspoon of vegetable detergent to the above solution. It's best and cheaper to use old newspapers or cloths instead of disposable paper towels to wipe the glass or mirror. You can also use this solution to clean and disinfect surfaces and, as we saw

before, for ironing, which also saves time and electricity.

Avoid using products that damage the environment since they will eventually affect our health or cause respiratory tract disorders and allergies. It's especially important to avoid chlorine, which is a carcinogen and yet, a product so widespread that unfortunately and inevitably, it ends up in our valuable aquifers. As a rule of thumb, avoid any product that claims to kill 99% of bacteria.

Avoid products that contain phthalates and synthetic fragrances. Remember that true cleanliness is when it does not smell bad. You do not have to smell perfume or fragrance. You can save a lot of money and improve your health and that of the planet if you prepare your own cleaning products. There are many easy recipes you can make with ingredients that you probably already have in your kitchen.

Save money using vinegar, baking soda, hydrogen peroxide, borax, and lemon to clean. Hydrogen peroxide is an excellent disinfectant and it is also a bleach. Or buy eco-friendly products following the guidelines below.

Making your own insecticides is easy and fast, also very economical. This is a partial list of some of the recipes that we present in section 7.10.

- Mosquito repellent
- Anti-flea mixture for dogs and cats
- Insecticide for ants and cockroaches

But if you do not have time to make your own cleaners or insecticides, there are products in local stores and in natural centers that are ecological. Make sure that the ingredients of these commercial products are vegetable-based and that they do not contain chemicals or fragrances. Many are well concentrated and therefore last longer, hence, saving money. Read the ingredients and check on EWG (ewg.org) or The Good Guide (goodguide.com) databases.

Bacteria are our Friends:
Most Bacteria are Good for us and Necessary for Life

Remember that some bacteria even prevent diseases such as: colon or vaginal infections, diarrhea, acne, psoriasis, bad smell (of the body and mouth), flu, colds, allergies, eczema, help lower bad cholesterol and are necessary for agriculture: they fix nutrients in the soil. In general, bacteria are beneficial or harmless, so ... why waste time and money to eliminate them?

7.7 Candles and Fragrance Diffusers

Another product that introduces toxins into our homes are candles and scented sprays or electric plugin diffusers. Almost all of these are made with petroleum-based, synthetic fragrances, and many candles also use wicks that contain lead. Many have been linked to allergies and asthma and are not safe, although they smell divine. So, listed here are three things to look for when shopping for candles. Make sure that:

1. The **scent** is derived from a natural source (from essential oils). If it says Fragrance and doesn't specify, it is most likely from a synthetic petroleum-based source.
2. The **wick** is made from cotton and lead-free
3. The **wax** should be soy-based, vegetable or beeswax, not paraffin or petroleum, and not a "blend".

Or better yet, create your own scents with essential oils. It's better to use an oil diffuser. They don't generate waste as candles do, and, on the long run, they are much cheaper given they use only a few drops of essential oils.

You can create your own aromatherapy mix with one (1) ounce of vodka or alcohol and 20 drops of essential oil. For example:

Relaxing oils use lavender, chamomile, rosemary.
Energizing oils, rosemary, bergamot, mint, orange, grapefruit.

But remember essential oils are very concentrated and must be diluted as explained above.

7.8 Why is indoor air so polluted?

Did you know that indoor air can be more polluted than the outdoor air? According to the EPA, one of the biggest health problems is indoor air quality. The level of pollutants in indoor air can be between 2 to 100 times higher than that of outdoor air. Why?

Due mainly to two factors; number one (1) the "smell of new", arises from the emissions of gases due to chemicals contained by products such as carpets, curtains, plastics, rubber, paint, glue. Many contain "VOC" (Volatile Organic Compounds), which have been linked to serious diseases.
The second (2) is the "smell of clean" to which we have become very accustomed. Regular cleaning products emit many harmful gases to our health, as we discussed above. Avoid ingredients such as triclosan, chloride, butoxyethanol, and limonene. Many also cause damage to the environment including fauna, flora, and the ozone layer, contributing to global warming.

7.9 Using Plants to Clean the Air

Do you know which plants have the greatest capacity to absorb toxins from the air? You can fill your home and office with these plants and let them clean the air for you. In addition, they will be regulating air humidity and providing oxygen.

Some plants have a more capable than others to clean the air. Some of the most effective in removing toxins are the given by this table below.

Plant Name	Chemical Vapors Removal Rating
Ferns : Nephrolepis Obliterata or Bostonian	9
Rubber Plant	9
Gerbera Daisy	9
Dwarf Date Palm	9
English Ivy	9
Bamboo Palm	9
Chrysanthemum	9
Dracaena or Dracaena Fragans	8
Peace Lily	8
Areca Palm	8
Ficus	8

Decorate your home and clean your air preventing diseases and allergies.

7.10   Ecological Insecticide Recipes

Learn how to make your own mosquito repellent, cockroach poison and cleaning products to keep your home sparkling!

To think that everything they sell in stores is healthy and safe for our health, is to be truly naive. But that's the way it should be in an ideal world. The reality is that many of the products we use at home contain chemicals that have not been tested to see if they are safe for humans.

They can be cheap, natural, and will not give you asthma. Use them to eliminate ants, lice, mites, mosquitoes, termites, and cockroaches in the home.
They are very economical and even more effective than commercial products.

Borax

Borax is a natural mineral that comes from a white stone and is used as a cleaning detergent to wash clothes and remove stains from dinnerware and pots. It is also an excellent insecticide!

Boric acid is derived from borax and it's more concentrated. Both are considered safe to use at home for the control of cockroaches and ants. Their chemical formula is NOT the same. Both are available at hardware stores and in some supermarkets, pharmacies, and department stores. You can use borax to spray on carpets where your dog sleeps and use it to wash it.

Prepare your own insecticide mix: (2 RECIPES)

Borax Insecticide:

Mix a teaspoon of borax with 2 of sugar and spread the powder along the way and corners where insects usually pass by and <u>out of the reach</u> of children and pets!

Boric acid Insecticide:

Dissolve 1 teaspoon (5mL) of boric acid powder and 10 teaspoons of sugar in 2 cups of water (500mL); wet cotton balls and leave them where insects frequent, such as inside the bathroom cabinets or behind the stove, and also out of the reach of children and pets.

Boric acid dehydrates the insects slowly and they do not notice it, so insects DO NOT develop immunity to it.

In addition, boric acid can be used as an antiseptic for minor wounds in a very diluted form, and for acne as it is naturally antibacterial. It has medicinal uses to treat fungi. It is also used to treat wood against termites.

Sprinkle this powder on the carpets to kill fleas, lice, and their eggs. It should not be ingested because it is TOXIC and some people's skin are sensitive to it, so wear gloves.

Cedarwood oil: A 1-ounce bottle last very long because its concentrated power. They also sell larger quantities to treat wood furniture and the wood outside the home.

Mosquito repellent: Dissolve 10-15 drops of Eucalyptus-lemon oil and 10 of cedarwood oil in a cup of water or alcohol and pour into a spray bottle. It gives a smell of wood that insects do not like. It is safe for children and pets, but do not spray on the eyes or near the mouth. It also relieves skin rash. You can add a few drops of peppermint oil, lavender or lemongrass, which increases they types of insects repelled.

Dust Mites on the bed: Spray the same repellent solution on the bed. Let it dry, it might smell like wood and oils for a few days. You can add droplets of pure peppermint or lavender oil which are also anti-germs and have a mild fragrance. Cedar oil kills mites that cause itching at night, mites feed on skin fragments released by humans on the mattress. It is also good to vacuum the mattress frequently.

Lice: Use the same mosquito repellent solution. Kills larvae and lice eggs. It does not cause irritation, asthma, or allergies, as it is not toxic to humans. It can be added to the shampoo and conditioner.

Fleas and ticks for Dogs: Use the same mosquito repellent solution in your dogs. You can add a few drops to the dog or cat shampoo. Do not spray cats with this liquid because cats lick themselves, and this oil is topical, it is not meant to be ingested. Yes, you can spray the dogs and where they lie down.

Fleas and ticks for Cats: Cats cannot eat peppermint oil, eucalyptus, pine, citrus, melaleuca, among others, because they can cause vomiting, and other health problems. For cats, use of solution of diluted oils of oregano, tarragon, cinnamon, clove and/or thyme.

Anti-flea collar: Make a mixture of droplets of essential oils of eucalyptus, tea tree, citronella, lavender and / or geranium and spread them on the cloth collar of your dog or cat.

Termites: Dissolve 1 teaspoon of cedar oil in 1/2 cup of lemongrass oil or other oil, and spray or apply with a brush on the wood to protect it from termites.

7.10.2 Pesticides for your Garden

Keep a garden free of insects without chemical poisons that kill insects and damage our health. There are many solutions offered by Organic Agriculture (see next chapter) but here I mention a few:

Thyme oil and cloves: Dissolve 10-15 droplets of thyme and cloves oil in 2 cups of water with a few drops of baking soda in a spray bottle. Spray leaves above and below.

Garlic, Onion, and hot pepper: Grind 1 head of garlic and a small onion. Add 1 tsp red pepper powder (cayenne) and mix with 1 quart of water. Soak for 1 hour or overnight, strain and add 1 tbsp. of ecological dishwashing liquid soap. Mix well.

Spray your plants where you have seen insects that eat leaves. Do not forget to use under the leaves. Store for 1 week in the fridge, labeled (so as not to be confused with salad dressing ☺)

Soda: Dissolve 1 tsp. of baking soda in 1 quart of warm water. Add 1 tsp of dishwashing soap (not detergent, but natural vegetable soap) so that the solution sticks to the leaves longer. Spray the plants well. Also works as a fungicide.

Garlic and oil: Soak 3 ounces of crushed garlic in 2 tsp. of oil for 24 hours. Add 1 pint of water and 1/4 ounce of liquid soap (not detergent) to wash dishes. Mix well and store in a jar. Combine 1-2 tbsp of this concentrate with 1 pint of water in a spray bottle. It is good for insects and as fungicide.

In fact, essential oils are so versatile I also use them for many natural health remedies. For instance, since clove oil has anti-viral properties, I slowly chew on one clove every time I feel like I'm about to get a cold when I feel an itchy throat. It is very spicy, but I move the clove oil with my tongue to the opening of my throat. It prevents me from getting sick in most cases. It also kills germs that cause bad breath, so I use it instead of chewing gum. I also use peppermint topically for headaches (a couple of drops on each side of my forehead) and many other ailments, in addition to all the cleaning and gardening applications.

So, whether you decide to use essential oils or other common products for controlling the insects in your house and garden, always remember **NOT to kill all insects!** Ladybugs and many other insects actually help your garden and farmers because they control insects that eat plants! We will discuss more on this subject on the next chapter.

8 SUSTAINABLE AGRICULTURE

Learn about the relationship between agriculture and global warming.

In this chapter we will learn what is sustainable agriculture and organic agriculture and how they differ from industrial or conventional agriculture.

8.1 Conventional Agriculture

Conventional agriculture, also known as **industrial agriculture**, refers to agricultural systems that include the use all or most of these:

- synthetic chemical fertilizers
- pesticides (including insecticides, fungicides, nematicides, etc.), herbicides and other continuous inputs
- genetically modified organisms (GMO)
- concentrated operations of animal feeding
- intensive irrigation
- intensive tillage
- monocultures

8.2 Sustainable Agriculture

Sustainable agriculture, according to the United Nations' Food and Agriculture Organization (FAO) is defined as the production of food, fibers or other vegetable or animal products that use agricultural techniques that protect the

- environment
- public health
- human communities
- and the welfare of animals.

Sustainable agriculture meets the needs of current generations without compromising future generations.

8.3 Organic Agriculture

Organic agriculture, as defined by FAO, depends more on ecosystem management than on external agricultural inputs.

- Considers the environmental and social impacts by **eliminating** the use of synthetic inputs, such as synthetic fertilizers and pesticides, veterinary drugs, genetically modified seeds and breeds, preservatives, additives, and irradiation.

- These are replaced by site-specific management practices that maintain and increase the long-term fertility of the soil and prevent pests and diseases.

According to the FAO/WHO Codex Alimentarius Commission, established in 1999 by representatives of 190 countries, organic agriculture is a holistic system of production management that promotes and improves the health of agroecosystems, including biodiversity, biological cycles, and biological activity of the soil, emphasizes the use of management practices preferably to the use of non-agricultural inputs. It also indicates that regional conditions require locally adapted systems, which is achieved by using, whenever possible, agronomic, biological, and mechanical methods, instead of using synthetic materials, to fulfill any specific function within the system.

8.3.1 Organic Agriculture Certification

The certification of farms as organic requires the approval from the USDA, in addition:

- It can be produced on vast industrial farms that may not be sustainable, while the sustainable ones are usually on small land.
- It does not necessarily comply with the welfare of the animals,
- Does not regulate the use of fossil fuels.

It also requires the payment of fees (application, inspections, etc.), which vary between $200 to $1500 depending on many factors.

In summary, when we talk about agriculture, the term organic means that it doesn't use agrochemicals. In addition, it uses no herbicides, pesticides, fungicides, insecticides, hormones, antibiotics, genetically modified organisms, and, in the case of animals, they are not confined to cages, but instead allowed to graze freely, i.e., free-range. The term *agroecology* also emphasizes the interdependent balance with the ecosystem. That's the way it was in the time of our grandparents. Everything back then was really natural and organic.

8.4 Agriculture and Global Warming

Many pesticides contain bromine which is 50 times more capable than CFC (chlorofluorocarbon) in breaking the ozone layer. This is the layer up in the atmosphere that protects us from UV solar radiation.
It should be mentioned that the CFC was banned in the 70s in a global agreement. However, they were replaced by gases such as HFC, which is a refrigerant that causes atmospheric warming.

Global warming also affects the ozone layer. It sends more water vapor to the stratosphere and when water molecules break down in the stratosphere, they release reactive hydrogen oxide molecules that destroy ozone molecules (O_3): creating a hole in the ozone layer.

In addition, synthetic fertilizers contain nitrous oxides (N_2O) which evaporate and are capable of absorbing between 215 to 300 times more heat (electromagnetic waves in the infrared range of the spectrum) than CO_2, thus augmenting global warming. As if that were not enough, many of these chemicals have been linked to several very serious diseases such as Parkinson's disease[41] and several types of cancer.[42].

Another aggravating factor is neonicotinoid; an ingredient in a common pesticide used in agriculture, which is also a neurotoxin, thus having the capability to affect our nervous system and potentially cause Alzheimer's and other brain diseases. Neonicotinoid pesticides damage the brain and the memory of bees and disorients them[43]. Bees are dying all over the world in large numbers, complete hives perish from one day to the next, in what is known as the Colony Collapse Disorder (CCD).

Bees are extremely important not only because they produce honey but because they pollinate 75% of plants. If we try to pollinate plants

---

[41] Widely used herbicide linked to cancer, Nature, March 2015

[42] Parkinson's disease and pesticides: what's the connection?, Scientific American, April 2014

[43] 18-Year Study links Neonicotinoids to Bee Colony Decline, Discover Magazine, Aug 2016.

by hand it would take an enormous amount of time and cost millions of dollars.

8.5 Fertilizer and NPK

Do you know what the numbers in 20-20-20 refer to in a fertilizer? They refer to the percentage of NPK: nitrogen, phosphorus, and potassium that the fertilizer contains. What does each one does and what are natural sources of them?

- **Nitrogen (N)**
  - ➤ Necessary for proteins, enzymes and metabolic processes in the synthesis and transfer of energy
  - ➤ It is part of the chlorophyll, the green pigment of the plant (photosynthesis)
  - ➤ It helps growth, increased production of seeds and fruits.
  - ➤ Improves the quality of leaf and forage crops

Natural sources include beans and *Arachis pintoi* or pinto peanuts, which is a forage plant: they trap N in the air and fix it into the roots thanks to bacteria in the soil.

Arachis pintoi provides nitrogen to the soil, prevents soil erosion, minimizes weeds, and serves as an ornament.

■ **Phosphorus (P)**

➢ It is an essential part of the process of photosynthesis
➢ Involved in the formation of all oils, sugars and starches
➢ Helps in the transformation of energy (solar to chemical)
➢ Promotes the maturation of the plant (to withstand stress)

- ➢ Effects rapid growth
- ➢ Encourages flowering and root growth

Natural sources include chicken manure, fish, bones, ashes, rock phosphate, alfalfa.

- ■ **Potassium (K)**

  - ➢ It is absorbed by plants in greater quantities than any other mineral element except N and Calcium
  - ➢ It helps in the development of proteins, photosynthesis, the amount of fruit yield, and the reduction of diseases.

Natural sources: leaves or compost from bananas and plantains, among others.

8.5.1 Compost

The composition of NPK came from a study done by Justus von Liebig in the 1800s. His contribution was very important for agriculture, however, a well-made compost has much more than NPK, it also contains micronutrients, carbon, hydrogen, cobalt, zinc, magnesium, and other components necessary for the plants to grow healthy.

In the list below, we see the various functions that some of these components have in the healthy growth of a plant.

Calcium (Ca)

> It is an essential part of the structure of the plant cell wall

> It offers normal transport and retention of other elements, as well as strength in the plant

> Counteracts the effect of alkali salts and organic acids within a plant

Magnesium (Mg)

> It is part of the chlorophyll in green plants and essential for photosynthesis

> Helps activate many plant enzymes necessary for growth

Sulfur (S)

> Essential to produce proteins

> Promotes the activity and development of enzymes and vitamins

> Helps in the formation of chlorophyll

> Improves root growth and seed production

> Helps with the vigorous growth of the plants (resistance to cold)

Other micronutrients include boron, copper, iron, molybdenum, and zinc.

There are many natural alternatives to agrochemicals such as those mentioned below.

- Use natural fertilizers (compost)
- Implement crop rotation (avoid monocultures)
- Use natural pesticides such as Neem oil

In fact, the FAO stated that organic agriculture is what has the potential to feed humanity in the future. It can help the economy of small farmers, benefit society and it's good for our climate. In the U.S., nearly 90% of all farms are constituted by small family farms, according to the

2016, 2017, and 2018 editions of the USDA Report titled "America's Diverse Family Farms".

A well-made compost does not burn the plant. Here we list some examples of sources of natural and economic fertilizers.

Worm composting
Also known as vermicomposting, worm poop can be easily maintained in a small container by feeding the worms with kitchen scraps such as banana peels, eggshells or vegetable and fruit

leftovers, tea bags, or paper (no gloss). You must minimize the amount of very acid produce like citrus fruits. The brown liquid is collected below in another container of the same size, through small opening from the top container. It is very concentrated and a very effective fertilizer.

Manure mostly from vegan animals such as cows and horses, or chickens (chicken manure) – Cure it before using it. It should not smell bad.

Vegetable scraps from the yard: such as grass, branches, dried leaves, eggs shells, hair, newspaper (if it has no chemical dyes)

Other such as coffee grounds, and even animal or human urine!

There are many videos available on the internet that show how to alternate layers of soil, garden waste, and kitchen waste to make compost. It also shows what to do and what not to do when creating your compost.

- www.youtube.com/watch?v=KsNYCb8nxqU
- www.elcalambrion.mrnatural.es/tag/agricultura-ecologica

8.5.4 Living Soil

Natural fertilizers keep the earth alive. This means that they do not kill the microorganisms that live in it such as: bacteria, insects, earthworms, and fungi, because they help agriculture.

The bacteria fix the nitrogen (N) in the soil, other microorganisms add nutrients, form a cycle with the plants and maintain the structure of the soil to allow the roots to grow easily. When using agrochemicals, the land becomes compact and sterile, making it hard for roots to grow. This soil then becomes addicted to agrochemicals.

Keeping the soil healthy while reducing greenhouse gases is also the focus of the so-called regenerative agriculture. Regenerative agriculture aims at tackling climate change by developing permaculture techniques that capture carbon into the soil while protecting the ecosystem. They promote the use of no-till farming, watershed improvement, cover cropping, and tree planting, among many other practices.

8.6 Controlling plagues

Many of these microorganisms found in the soil even help control pests in the field. In addition, there are other ways to control them without toxic agrochemicals.

But it is essential to distinguish harmful insects from those beneficial to agriculture. Crop rotation is also used (so that the soil recovers nutrients used by different crops).

Lemongrass can be used for tea and also to repel ants and other pests, so it's a good idea to plant it next to plants that attract insects.

Another reason to avoid monocultures is that they make crops more vulnerable to pests. You can plant herbs that repel insects such as lemongrass and chrysanthemum next to your crops. Regarding Fungicides and Pesticides, several natural mixtures can be used, such as those based on the Neem, geranium, thyme, and clover essential oils.

Another common mixture is onions, garlic, and vegetable dishwashing liquid soap. (Chop the onions and garlic). A mixture of soda powder and oil with hot pepper (chili peppers are poured)

essential oils such as Neem, cloves, geranium, garlic, onion, lemongrass, and earth carnations, among others. In addition, there are commercially available products that use ecological ingredients.

8.6.1 Animals that Help Agriculture

Keep in mind that many animals are actually "friends" of agriculture and orchards. For example, bees, bats, and birds do the work of pollinating plants, which is necessary for many varieties of plants to bear fruit. Boas and hawks eat rats. Ants and earthworms maintain the structure of the soil so that water flows and the roots grow.

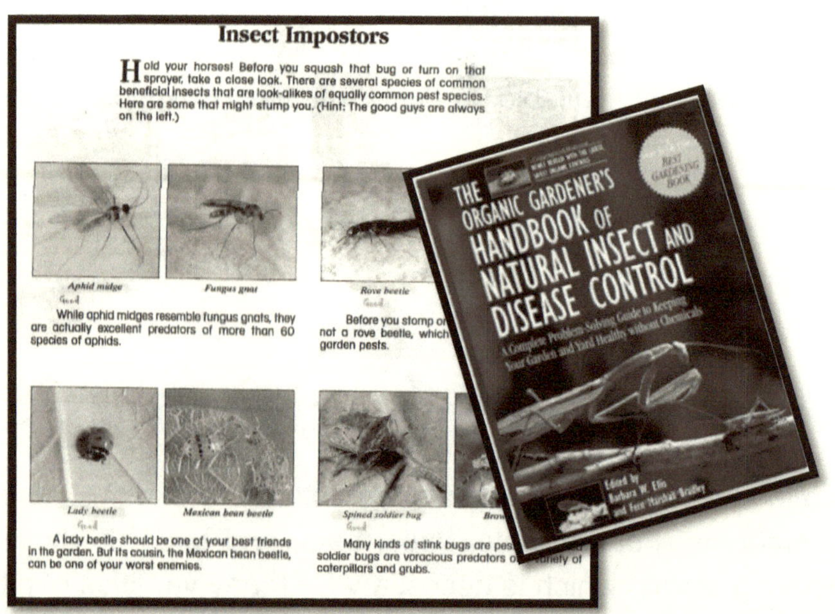

These images above are from Barbara W. Ellis and Fern Marshall Bradley's book, "*The Organic Gardener's Handbook of Natural Insect and Disease Control: A Complete Problem-Solving Guide to Keeping Your Garden and Yard Healthy Without Chemicals.*" It presents some of the insects that are beneficial for agriculture and those that resemble it. They are examples of insect "impostors". This is an excellent reference for organic farmers. Another excellent reference but available only in Spanish is Nelson Alvarez-Febles, "*El Huerto Casero. Manual De Agricultura Orgánica*".

The insects shown on the right are beneficial or harmless to agriculture, while those on the left are harmful. That is why it is important not to use a synthetic insecticide because it kills all insects indiscriminately and even pollinators. Without pollinators there are no fruits!

8.6.2 Synthetic pesticides
and other agrochemicals and their effect on health

Why should we avoid synthetic pesticides and other agrochemicals? What adverse effects do they have? Many agrochemicals contain toxins that contaminate the soil and travel through the root up toward the produce, also contaminating the fruits and vegetable harvested. In addition, they contaminate bodies of water because when it rains, it infiltrates into the rivers, lakes, and even seas. This affects fishing and other wildlife and gives rise to algae blooms. There are regions where millions of fish have appeared dead due to the discharge of agrochemicals by the rivers.

Another harmful effect is on our health: many of the herbicides contain neurotoxins, for example, some are derived from the agent orange that was used during the Vietnam war. Neurotoxins attack the brain and can cause ailments such as Parkinson's disease. In addition, the Roundup® herbicide contains an ingredient, c called **glyphosate**, that was cataloged in 2015 by WHO as a probable carcinogen for humans. This is consistent with a 2013 study at MIT that establishes a relationship between the Roundup (from the Monsanto company) and diseases such as cancer, Parkinson's, and others. Moreover, as we mentioned, some contain bromide which damages the ozone layer.

One of the common ingredients in synthetic fertilizers used in agriculture today is nitrous oxide. These also cause diseases, allergies, and damage to the respiratory system. Similarly, as we mentioned earlier, they cause global warming.

8.7 Are organic products healthier?

According to several studies in 2007 and 2014, including one published in British Journal of Nutrition, organic products are healthier because they contain more antioxidants. It is thought that the plant produces antioxidants to be able to repel insects, which does not happen in plants irrigated with chemical insecticides. Jane Goodall in her book Reason for Hope, mentioned that orangutans prefer organic fruits when they are given a choice, probably because they have a much more sensitive sense of smell than humans do.

Something that is often overlooked when we want to have an organic garden at home is the use of hygiene products close to the orchard, garden or the farmland. We should not for example clean a terrace with chloride or other strong detergents if then with the hose the water runs to the ground where vegetables are grown. In the case of chloride, it has been linked to cancer in animal studies as mentioned previously. Another habit that should be avoided is smoking since each cigarette has thousands of toxins that penetrate the soil and roots, as we further explain in the section. The same applies to all personal hygiene products, choose those that are plant-base, not petroleum, as we mentioned in chapter 7.

8.8 Smoking, agriculture, and climate change

Did you know that smoking affects the planet and agriculture?

Here we list some of the effects of cigarette butts:

1. Deforestation; one tree is lost for every 300 cigarettes.
2. Contamination of fauna, flora, and water with over 4,000 toxins secreted by millions of cigarette butts. It is impossible to have an organic garden if there are butts in the ground.
3. The use of agrochemicals for tobacco plants is very common and harmful.
4. Fires: 1/4 to 1/3 of all fires in the United States are caused by cigarette butts. This includes deaths and property damage.
5. Second-hand Smoking affects the health of others and pollutes the air.
6. The packing and drying processes consume a lot of paper, which implies even more deforestation.
7. In addition, the economic cost is increasing.
8. Carcinogens inside cigarettes go to your body and to your family members; to fauna and flora.
9. The butts are garbage that cannot be recycled, which constitutes anywhere from 10% to 36% of garbage depending on the region. Every year 1,700 million pounds of butts are produced around the world.

Finally, it is important to mention the adverse effect of burning waste in your yard or farm, even if it is a vegetation fire. Firstly, in many states to burn materials in your yard, you need a permit from the local fire department. Secondly, smoke causes pollution in the air and therefore causes similar damage as cigarette smoke such as asthma, emphysema, bronchitis, and lung cancer. Thirdly, fires are dangerous and also increase the emissions of greenhouse gases that contribute to global warming and climate change. What alternatives exist to the burning of pastures and vegetable waste? You can make compost instead with any vegetable waste and you will have an excellent fertilizer for your plants. You can also use a special type of mower that chops branches, clippings, and other farm waste so they integrate into the soil, recycling the materials, instead of starting a fire; be considerate to others.

8.9 FAO Report with regards to Agriculture

In its report entitled World Food Summit Report of 2007, the FAO strongly affirms that organic agriculture can address local and global food security challenges. It also remarks that the organic market rose from $40 billion in 2006, $70 billion in 2012. In addition, it mentions other advantages such as minimize air, soil, and water pollution, and optimize the health and productivity of plants, animals, and people. Among its strongest benefits, the FAO mentions that organic agriculture does not depend on fossil fuels. All these factors make the impact to the environment minimal and for this reason it is profitable. It reminds us that organic agriculture combines modern science and indigenous knowledge.

In summary, the FAO report strongly suggests that a global change towards organic agriculture can combat world hunger and, at the same time, tackle climate change.

9 EATING TO STOP GLOBAL WARMING

Eating to stop climate change benefits you.

When you learn to select food that helps curb global warming, you obtain so many advantages that you will wonder, how could you live so long without making the change? Among other things you will gain:

- Health (for example, it lowers your chances of getting cancer, diabetes, heart disease, among others.)
- Energy and quality of life
- Maintain an adequate weight without going hungry
- It can be economical saving about $ 750 per person per year.[44]

You will also gain regularity: a healthy person is supposed to evacuate 3 times a day. Constipation has been linked to colon cancer.

9.1 Guide to eating ecologically

Actually, it is not a diet but a lifestyle. The goal is to create healthy habits. It can be summarized in seven words: Eat less, be healthier and move more.

---

[44]blogs.elnuevodia.com/ahorros-verdes/2018/02/05/come-para-frenar-el-calentamiento-global-y-ahorra-750-al-ano-por-persona/

Follow these 9 guides of what to eat to improve your health and that of the planet.

9.1.1 Avoid individual and canned packages

One of the first things to avoid is individually packaged products and canned products. Products sold in individual packages cost up to 5 times more than products prepared at home. The same happens with

canned goods. Convenience costs money and generates much more waste, and many times these products come in containers that cannot be recycled everywhere, such as tin cans or non-recyclable plastics. Instead of buying canned beans and other canned vegetables, it is much cheaper to buy them raw and cook them at home.

In addition, cans and pots have traces of aluminum linked to Alzheimer's disease. Aluminum is a neurotoxin and accumulates in the brain. Furthermore, the white lining inside cans contains BPA (Bisphenol A); this chemical has been linked to diabetes, obesity, and other diseases because it mimics human hormones.

You save a lot of money: For example, cooked dry beans cost about half price compared to canned.

9.1.2 Consume local and natural products

Local implies less transportation to your home, decreasing CO_2 emissions. It helps the economy of your town or county. On the other hand, local products are fresher and with more nutrients than canned products which usually travel thousands of miles before reaching your home. Visit agroecological markets near you. Some offer monthly delivery services.

9.1.3 Consume whole foods

Another essential point to reduce the impact of what we eat is to consume unrefined products. The energy needed to refine products contributes greatly to the amount of gas emissions that heat the atmosphere and the planet.

In addition, processing removes most of the nutrients and fiber from our food, which are essential for good nutrition.

Therefore, whenever you have a choice, choose brown rice, 100% whole wheat flour, whole wheat pasta, turbinado sugar, and so on.

Look at the next graph, which compares the amount of nutrients and fiber in white bread versus whole wheat bread. It's as if the whole wheat flour came with natural vitamins & minerals supplement!

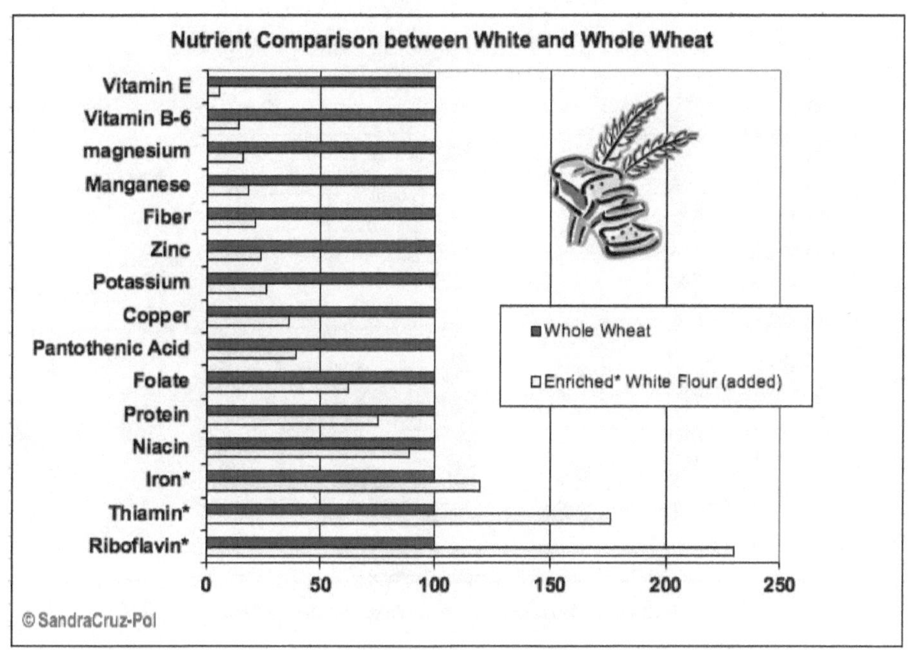

The same goes for brown rice; it needs less energy to process and has many more nutrients than white rice as shown in the following graphs.

White rice and white bread are what we call "empty calories" because they have calories, but the body is left without most of the nutrients, and this is despite the fact that the flour is "enriched" with vitamins (many times synthetic versions of vitamins) that are added to replace part of what's lost in the refining process. Many synthetic vitamins and nutrients are not digested so efficiently by our bodies as natural versions are.

As seen in this graph, 100% whole wheat bread is much more nutritious than white wheat bread. "Whole white" bread, is also refined, so it is not good for your health or the planet.

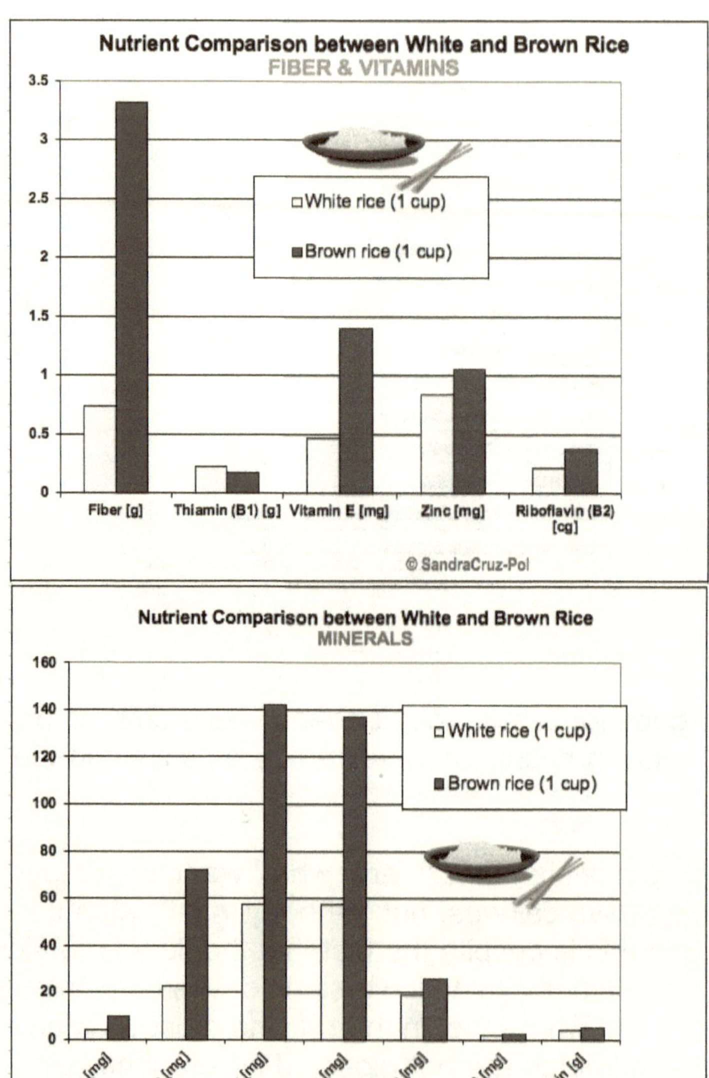

Comparison of fiber, vitamins (top graph) and minerals (bottom graph) content between refined and whole rice.

Brown rice is cooked differently than white rice. The first time I tried to cook brown rice it was awful because I didn't follow the package instructions. Now is perfect every time. You only need to stir it for 1 minute at the beginning in boiling water, then it is covered and simmered in low heat for 35 minutes, and presto! It has a more robust flavor; you will learn to love it.

9.1.4 Eat Natural

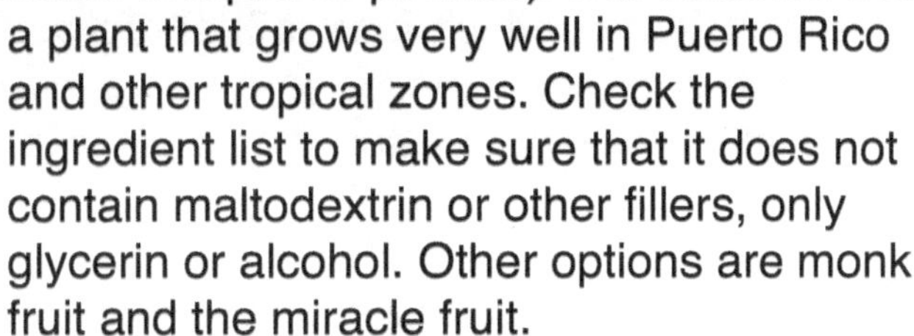

Most artificial ingredients are usually derived from petroleum! These are usually hidden in the ingredients list using names that are similar to the natural ingredient. For example, instead of sucrose, which is natural, we get sweeteners like Sucralose (brand-named Splenda), Corn Syrup, or HFCS, which stands for High Fructose Corn Syrup. Likewise, for artificial colors and flavors.

Some of these artificial ingredients are known to be potential carcinogens, others have not been studied well. A natural option for diabetics is Stevia (available in liquid or powder). It is obtained from a plant that grows very well in Puerto Rico and other tropical zones. Check the ingredient list to make sure that it does not contain maltodextrin or other fillers, only glycerin or alcohol. Other options are monk fruit and the miracle fruit.

Avoid also artificial flavors and colors like Vanillin and use pure vanilla extract instead. Note that if you buy vanilla very cheap like the one you get sometimes in several Caribbean islands, it's probably vanillin, not vanilla). Real vanilla is made from the thin pod of an orchid, and that is why is expensive to produce. In fact, the word vanilla comes from the translation of "tiny pod" in Spanish, ("vainilla" or "vaina chiquita").

The production of corn syrup also greatly damages the environment during its planting and production stages.[45]
Corn syrup is a highly processed product that converts part of the corn glucose into fructose and has a very harmful effect on the planet. Around 90% of corn is GMO[46] (except some corn species such as blue corn and corn that is used for popcorn, those are not yet GMO)[47], and uses many herbicides and other agrochemicals for its production. In addition, it uses many resources such as energy, water, and land.

Several studies including at U.C. Davis, have established a relationship between the consumption of Corn Syrup and pancreatic cancer, diabetes, obesity, and cardiovascular diseases.

Thanks to federal subsidies, the price of corn syrup is much lower than that of sugar, which makes it attractive for the food industry to increase their profits. Hence, corn syrup is found in a large number of products, including breads, some of which claim to be "Healthy" on the label.

Some breads contain an ingredient that is used to make yoga mats spongy. It's called azodicarbonamide (abbreviated azod) and is used

---

[45] www.cancer.gov/cancertopics/factsheet/Risk/artificial-sweeteners

[46] www.ewg.org/enviroblog/2014/04/corn#.W0jBUNgzqnc

[47] https://www.mommypotamus.com/got-the-blues-about-gmo-corn-two-varieties-remain-uncontaminated/

to condition the bread dough. It is banned in Europe and Australia. In the U.S., Subway restaurants stopped using this ingredient in their loaves after an online petition by Vani Hari in 2014, but it's still used in some fast food restaurants (Ask for a list of ingredients). A study published in 2011 by the Journal of Agriculture and Food Chemistry, states that azod has been linked to cancer and tumor development[48]. However, the FDA believes that low levels of azod are harmless to our health.

As we mentioned earlier, it is completely legal to put almost anything on the front of the label. The only thing regulated by law is the list of ingredients. A very common case, is a cereal that indicates on the cover that it's a blueberries and pomegranate cereal, however, does not contain any of these fruits among its ingredients [49].

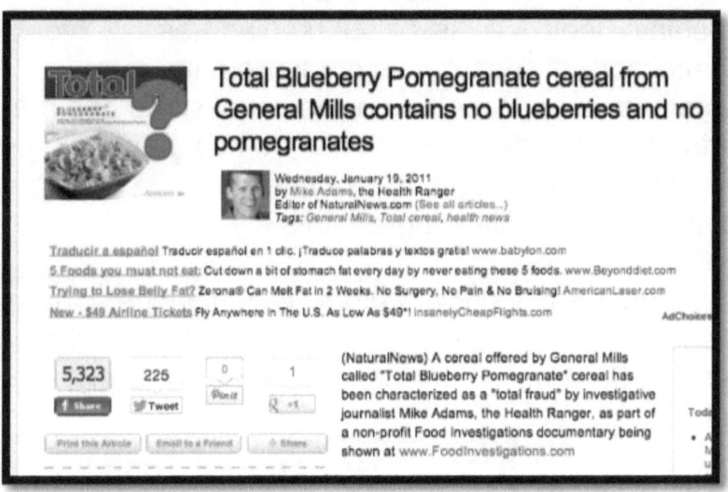

Total Blueberry Pomegranate cereal from General Mills contains no blueberries and no pomegranates

Wednesday, January 19, 2011
by Mike Adams, the Health Ranger
Editor of NaturalNews.com (See all articles...)
Tags: General Mills, Total cereal, health news

Traducir a español Traducir español en 1 clic. ¡Traduce palabras y textos gratis! www.babylon.com
5 Foods you must not eat: Cut down a bit of stomach fat every day by never eating these 5 foods. www.Beyonddiet.com
Trying to Lose Belly Fat? Zerona® Can Melt Fat In 2 Weeks. No Surgery, No Pain & No Bruising! AmericanLaser.com
New - $49 Airline Tickets Fly Anywhere In The U.S. As Low As $49*! InsanelyCheapFlights.com

AdChoices

5,323   225   0   1

(NaturalNews) A cereal offered by General Mills called "Total Blueberry Pomegranate" cereal has been characterized as a "total fraud" by investigative journalist Mike Adams, the Health Ranger, as part of a non-profit Food Investigations documentary being shown at www.FoodInvestigations.com

---

[48] www.ncbi.nlm.nih.gov/pubmed/21786817
[49] www.law360.com/ar9cles/278972/general-mills-dodges-total-cereal-false-labeling-suit

On the other hand, be cautious with the word NATURAL. The word "natural" is not regulated by FDA so it does not really mean anything. Even petroleum can be considered natural! Therefore, don't be fooled by the front of the labels. Read the ingredients and avoid:

- **Sucralose** is artificially produced in laboratories and its name is very similar to the natural sweetener, sucrose.
- **Carmine** are reddish insects, a Mexican beetle called cochineal (cochineal bug) where the female is brown, but the male is an intense shade of red. It is used in many restaurants and companies to make frappe of strawberries and red velvet cake.
- **Shellac =** Another example of insects is Shellac, commonly used as nail polish. It is also used to give chocolates and candy a shiny look. It is also known as "Confectioners Glaze". It is made from the secretions of an insect during its larval stage and may contain parts of their bodies. It is cataloged as a natural ingredient. 
- Always avoid products that say "Light" or "Diet", they usually have many unhealthy ingredients.

Another example are artificial colors. For instance, Caramel Color found in sodas has can be a potential carcinogen depending on where you live. Caramel color is used for many desserts, breads and soft drinks.

There are four types of caramel color. The cheapest one, called 4-Mei, is an ingredient cataloged

Consumer Reports: Too many sodas contain potential carcinogen

By **William Hudson**, CNN

January 23, 2014 -- Updated 1449 GMT (2249 HKT)

as a potential carcinogenic. The FDA does not require industries to indicate on the label which type of caramel color is used, so most companies choose to use the cheapest.

Within the U.S., only in California regulates the level of 4-Mei. Therefore, the same product is identified with a code on the label to know where it can be sold. The one that arrives in California must contain a much smaller level of ingredients that cause cancer than the one that arrives at Puerto Rico, New York and other states. The Consumer's Report magazine has several reports on this from 2013 and 2015.

It is preferable to consume what is closest to its natural state. For example, learn to know the difference between butter and margarine. Most margarines contain 'trans fats' which have been linked to heart disease and raise cholesterol, and often have many synthetic ingredients.

Butter contains only one ingredient, it does not contain artificial products, so it is preferable to margarine. However, keep in mind that it is an animal fat, so it must be consumed in moderation. It is better to use coconut oil, which lowers the bad cholesterol and raises the good cholesterol[50].

---

[50] Dayrit, C. S., "COCONUT OIL: Atherogenic or Not? ", Philippine Journal of Cardiology July-September 2003, Volume 31 Number 3:97-104

Fats are necessary for the body; they help in many body functions and also help assimilate other nutrients. Nonetheless, you should always consume fats in moderation. Healthy fats include avocado, walnuts, almonds, and sunflower seeds, among others.

We will examine the healthiest oils in section 9.1.10. Also, choose natural colors made of vegetables and fruits. The page Naturallysavvy.com provides a list of the ingredients that we should avoid and for each one indicates the health risks.

9.1.5 Organic Produce

Organic products are planted as they were thousands of years ago, without agrochemicals (synthetic fertilizers, pesticides, herbicides, fungicides, or genes from other organisms (GMO, which have been linked to tumors and genetic defects).

Many small farmers use organic agriculture practices but do not have the organic agriculture certification. The price of organic produce will go down when the government transfers the subsidies and incentives currently given to industrial agriculture companies, toward organic agriculture farmers.

Industrial agriculture uses synthetic fertilizers, pesticides, and other toxic agrochemicals.

Here is a list of produce that are commonly GMO: 90% of corn, soy, canola, beets, and papayas. The same happens with the pineapples of Hawaii. Unfortunately, this is not indicated by the label nor on the UPC bar code number.

Canola oil means Canadian Oil Low Acid. It was designed in Canada of a very acid and toxic oil (rapeseed oil) that is inedible, so they process it to remove the acid, and it is almost always genetically modified. Canola oil is reduced in erucic acid, it only contains about 2%. In Europe, canola oil is produced only from plants that are not genetically modified, but in the U.S., the majority (90%) of that oil is transgenic (GMO).

To extract Canola oil high temperatures and a toxic solvent called hexane are used, then bathed in sodium hydroxide to remove wax, then whiten and then reheated using steam injection. It is a very complicated process compared to how olive oil or other plants are obtained.

Since 1995 Monsanto modified Canola oil to resist large amounts of Roundup herbicide. In fact, most commercialized GMO produce are modified to have glyphosate-resistance, thus increasing the use of this herbicide, polluting the soil and rivers. The herbicide has been linked to cancer by the WHO. According to a 2019 study published in Mutation Research journal, it raises cancer risk by 41% [51]. I prefer to use natural options with 0% erucic acid (linked to heart disease).

---

[51] Zhang, et al., Exposure to Glyphosate-Based Herbicides and Risk for Non-Hodgkin Lymphoma: A Meta-Analysis and Supporting Evidence, Mutation Research, Feb 2019.

Learn which products to buy organic; this list shows the products commonly found with most pesticides in tests.

> **Produce that normally contain large amounts of agrochemicals:**
> Apples, Grapes, Strawberries, Lettuce, Celery, Green peppers, Dairy products, Potatoes, Tomatoes.

Consequently, it's worth investing money to buy them organic. Apples, for example, usually have traces of up to 6 different pesticides. They are also usually covered with a layer of petroleum wax to make them shine and last longer. You must remove it with a brush and hot water or peel the apple before eating.

Quite the reverse, the following produce usually do not contain many traces of pesticides. Thus, you can save money and buy these conventionally (not organic).

> **Produce that normally don't have pesticides:**
> Bananas, Oranges, Tangerines, Grapefruits, Melons, Avocados, Pineapples, Onions, and Mangos.

Now, just because a product says it's organic, does not mean it's necessarily healthy. For example, a sponge cake, high sugar cookies, and other pre-cooked foods may be organic, but contain too much salt, fat, and carbohydrates. Check the ingredients.

9.1.6 Safe Cooking utensils

Most people who want to be healthy forget a super important detail: **Where you cook and serve food is as important as the ingredients you use.**

What good is it to buy the healthiest ingredients in the world if you cook them in utensils that infiltrate toxins to your food?

Use healthy utensils such as those made with bamboo, clay, Pyrex® or cooking glass, stainless steel, silicone, ceramic, Corning®, and iron pots. It's important to use dinnerware that is lead-free and cadmium-free. In California, **Proposition 65** (Prop65) requires businesses to provide warnings about significant exposures to chemicals that cause cancer, birth defects or other reproductive harm.

Silicone is a mix of natural silicon and molecules of oxygen, and other ingredients such as hydrogen, carbon, and methyl chloride. Studies show it doesn't leach chemicals to your food when used cold. It does leach small amounts of certain compounds called siloxanes when exposed to both fat and temperatures over 300F.[52]

----

[52] www.ncbi.nlm.nih.gov/pmc/articles/PMC4884743/
www.thetot.com/baby/is-silicone-safe/
https://masonbottle.com/blogs/news/49464836-is-silicone-really-safe-will-i

Pressure cookers help save time and electricity, but never use pressure cookers made of aluminum, use stainless steel type only. It takes only about 15 minutes in total to soften and stew beans and grains previously soaked in water a few hours. These cookers also save water. Another good choice are iron pans, they were the non-stick pans of our grandmothers! In addition, they also save energy since they get so hot, that they should only be used in low or medium heat.

In order for the iron pan to work as a non-stick, follow the instructions to learn how to season it, so that it creates a non-stick surface. It is very easy to clean, just wipe with a napkin, cloth, or sponge and dry after each use. You can also wash it with warm water and soap and heat with high smoking point oil for 15-20 minutes on top of the stove. It can be used for stir-fry, fry eggs, and make pancakes, among other dishes, and can last for generations. Even if it rusts, 
it can be easily restored and seasoned. It infiltrates iron into your

food, which is a good thing. They are very heavy, which helps build muscles and keep your arms toned.

It is important for your health to avoid containers and pots made of aluminum, foam, Teflon, and plastic in your kitchen, even if plastic containers say, "Microwave Safe". That only means that it will not melt, but it still leaches toxic chemicals into your food. These materials contain some or all of the following chemicals: BPA, phthalates, and antimony which infiltrate your drink and food. Teflon begins to infiltrate chemicals into the food as soon as it has a small scratch.

Styrene or polystyrene (microscopic chains of several molecules of styrene) has been linked to several diseases because the styrene molecules leach into the food and enter your system and can then affect your liver and it could even cause cancer[53]. And as if this was not enough reason to stop using them, these materials are also difficult or impossible to recycle, and thus remain eternally in nature polluting our environment and entering our food chain.

9.1.7 Eco-friendly Alternatives to Frying

In Puerto Rico as in most countries it is very difficult to recycle cooking oil and most people end up throwing it down the sink! Just one gallon of oil can contaminate up to 1 million gallons of water! On top of this, oils are expensive and fried food is not healthy. The best

---

[53] The Department of Health and Human Services (DHHS), National Toxicology Program (NTP) listed styrene as "reasonably anticipated to be a human carcinogen" , Report on Carcinogens, Twelfth Edition, June 10, 2011.

alternative to frying is to bake or sauté. This minimizes the use of oil. You will also save money on oil and medicines related to high fat consumption (diabetes, obesity, and heart disease).

What are the best oils? Use peanut oil, virgin olive oil, coconut oil or sunflower oil for cooking because they can resist higher temperatures before burning (high smoking point). And then use regular olive oil, hemp, or flaxseed for salads, but not for cooking. All are very healthy and enhance the flavor of your meals.

- Avoid corn, soybean, and canola oil. Almost all of these oils are GMO which contain large amounts of herbicides and have been linked to tumors in laboratory rats. Between 70-90% of these oils are genetically modified?[54]
  - The American Academy of Environmental Medicine (AAEM) urges doctors to recommend non-GMO diets to their patients.[55]

9.1.8 Reduce or Eliminate Meat Consumption

This is the most important point for the planet and the one that will bring you more health, although it may be the most challenging. You can do it gradually or overnight, whatever works best for you.

It is the most important of all changes in your diet for the planet given that according to several studies including one by the United Nations

---

[54]http://www.huffingtonpost.com/margie-kelly/genetically-modified-food_b_2039455.html

[55] http://www.aaemonline.org/gmopost.html

in 2006 *"raising animals for consumption generates more greenhouse gases than ALL cars and trucks in the world, combined'*.

A more recent report indicates that 51% of greenhouse gases are produced by the consumption of meat (World Watch, 2012).

Meat consumption and cancer

However, there are many myths and misinformation regarding meat consumption. First you must understand that humans do not need any meat to have good health, on the contrary! The consumption of meat, especially red and processed meat, has been linked to several types of cancer and heart disease.

This is what the experts have to say:

"Meat Consumption is Linked to Increased Risk of Colon Cancer."-Harvard Medical School" [56]

"Red Meat Lovers have more Liver Cancer" - National Institute of Health [57]

"Red meat is linked to bowel cancer"–UK Dept. of Health [58]

"The consumption of red and processed meat and the risk of cancer of the pancreas"- British Journal of Cancer [59].

---

[56] http://www.health.harvard.edu/

[57] http://www.nlm.nih.gov

[58] U.K. Cancer Research www.dh.gov.uk, www.cancerresearchuk.org/cancer-info/cancerstats/types/bowel/riskfactors/bowel-cancer-risk-factors

[59] British Journal of Cancer (2012) 106, 603–607 www.nature.com/bjc/journal/v106/n3/full/bjc2011585a.html

The Protein's Myth

Did you know that four of the top five death-causing diseases in the
United States and Puerto Rico are linked to high-protein diets? [61] [62]
Did you know that an average adult only needs about 0.36 gr/lb of
protein daily? [63] This equals to about 40-50 grams of required daily
protein for the average person. On average people consume more
than 120 g daily!

Furthermore, you can get all your proteins, amino acids, and vitamins
(except vitamin B12 which is only produced by a bacteria) from plant
sources such as grains, nuts, soybeans, quinoa, sesame, spirulina,
seaweed, hemp, eggs (organic, free-range), asparagus, chia,
pumpkin, and sunflower seeds, broccoli, lentils, peas and so many
others. Quinoa is a cereal that is cooked in a similar way as rice and
was used by the Incas in South America for thousands of years. You
can get Vitamin B12 from yeast products such as Marmite or
Vegemite spread.

> **The fact that Vitamin B12 is only produced by
> a type of bacteria is another reason to avoid
> cleaners that claim to kill all bacteria.**

---

[60]www.sciencedaily.com/releases/2008/11/081113181428.htm

[61] www.ncbi.nlm.nih.gov/books/NBK235012/

[62] www.empr.com/news/cdc-5-leading-causes-of-death-in-the-us/article/573917/

[63]www.aarp.org/health/healthy-living/info-2018/protein-needs-fd.html?intcmp=AE-
HEA-HL-EOA1

When I stopped eating red meat, pork, and poultry over 3 decades ago, many people told me that I would not find the necessary proteins to be healthy. Nonetheless, there are many cultures that have never consumed meat and are healthy. Actually, I felt more energized than ever before, lighter.

A recent study has identified several regions on the planet, called the Blue Zones, where people are healthy and active until around 100 years old. All these zones have three factors in common: they live active lives, exercising daily, have a mostly plant-based diet, and cultivate a sense of community and spirituality.

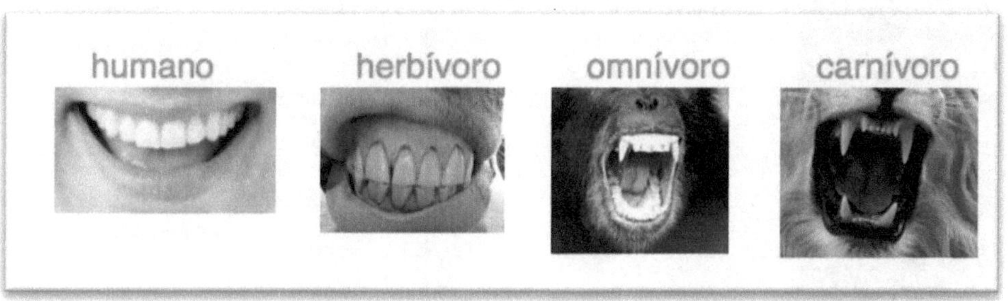

Comparison of the teeth of various types of animals.

If we compare our dentures with that of carnivorous and omnivorous animals such as lions and bears, or herbivores, such as deer, we will realize that our teeth were designed for the consumption of vegetables. The table below is adapted from "The Comparative Anatomy of Eating" by Milton R. Mills, M.D. and summarized on MichaelBlueJay.com http://michaelbluejay.com/veg/natural.html.

Humas are biologically designed to be Vegetarians (Herbivorous)			
	Carnivorous	**Omniovrous**	**Herbivores**	**Humans**
---	---	---	---	---
Chewing	None: swalllows food whole	Swalllows food whole and/or simple crushing	Extensive chewing necessary	Extensive chewing necessary
Length of small intestine	3-6 times body length	4-6 times body length	10-12+ times body length	10-11 times body length
Facial muscles	Reduced to allow wide mouth gape	Reduced	Well-Developed	Well-Developed
Liver	Can detoxify vitamin A	Can detoxify vitamin A	Cannot detoxify vitamin A	Cannot detoxify vitamin A
Stomach acidity with food in stomach	≤ pH 1	≤ pH 1	pH 4-5	pH 4-5
Kidney	Extremely concentrated urine	Extremely concentrated urine	Moderately concentrated urine	Moderately concentrated urine
Nails	Sharp claws	Sharp claws	Flattened nails or blunt hooves	Flattened nails
Saliva	No digestive enzymes	No digestive enzymes	Carbohydrate digesting enzymes	Carbohydrate digesting enzymes
Colon	Simple, short, and smooth	Simple, short, and smooth	Long, complex; may be sacculated	Long; sacculated
Jaw	Angle not expanded	Angle not expanded	Expanded angle	Expanded angle
Jaw joint location	On same plane as molar teeth	On same plane as molar teeth	Above the plane of the molar	Above the plane of the molar
Jaw motion	Shearing minimal side-to-side motion	Shearing minimal side-to-side motion	No shear: good side-to-side front-to-back	No shear: good side-to-side front-to-back
Major jaw muscle	Temporalis	Temporalis	Masseter and ptergoids	Masseter and ptergoids
Mouth opening vs. head size	Large	Large	Small	Small
Teeth: Incisors	Short and pointed	Short and pointed	Broead, flattend and spade-shaped	Broead, flattend and spade-shaped
Teeth: Canines	Long, sharp, and curved	Long, sharp, and curved	Dull and sort or long (for defense), or none	Short and blunted
Teeth: Molars	Sharp, jagged and blade-shaped	Sharp blades and/or flatted	Flattened with cusps vs. complex surface	Flattened with nodular cusps

As summarized on the table, the same conclusion is found if we compare other characteristics of the animal kingdom such as the PH level in the stomach, the length of the intestine, and many other biological characteristics; they all point to the fact that humans were designed to be vegetarians.[64]

---

[64] *The Comparative Anatomy of Eating*, by Milton R. Mills

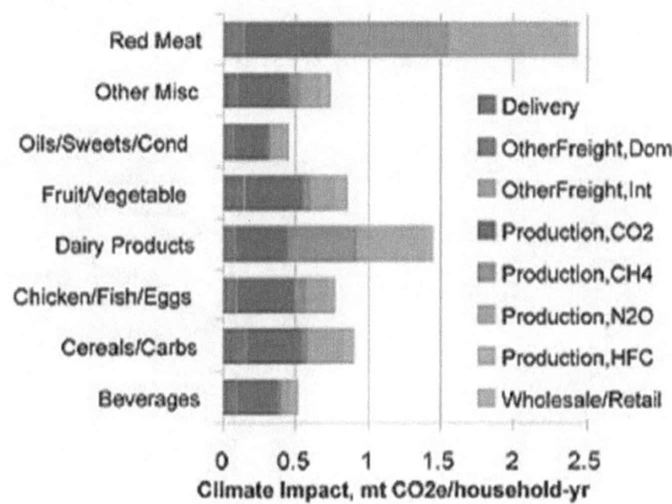

Total GHG emissions linked to household food consumption in the US, and the climate impacts of different food groups. [Credit: Weber, C. L., and H. S. Matthews, 2008: Food-Miles and the Relative Climate Impacts of Food Choices in the United States. Environmental Science & Technology]

The bars in this graph summarize how various diets contribute to greenhouse gas emissions. The gases emitted include those related to methane (CH_4), transportation, refrigeration, processing, and agrochemicals. For example, N_2O are produced from synthetic fertilizers. This chart does not include water or the use of terrain, which we will present later.

The combination of many factors is what makes meat consumption unsustainable due to the high use of resources and excessive emissions. The impact of red meat consumption is almost 2.5 million metric tons of greenhouse gases, compared to less than 0.8 for cereals and fruits.

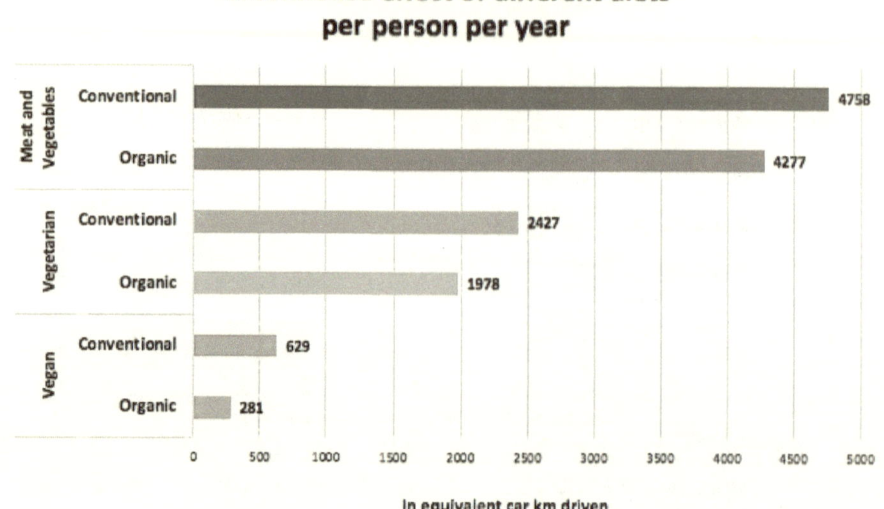

Figure 9.1 Adapted from Foodwatch Report on the Effects of GHG from Agriculture available on https://www.L214.com

This graph adapted from the FoodWatch 2002 Report [65] shows the effect on the planet of meat consumption in Germany. It takes into consideration the use of water, deforestation, refrigeration, and transportation, among other factors. We can conclude that an organic and vegan diet (vegetarian without dairy products), is the one with the least emissions of greenhouse gases.

---

[65] www.foodwatch.org/uploads/media/foodwatch_report_on_the_greenhouse_effe ct_of_farming_05_2009_01.pdf

Among all animal meats, fish has the least impact on the planet, except for some species such as salmon grown in tanks. In order from higher to lower emissions, we find beef, farmed crustaceans, lamb, mutton, dairy, pig, poultry, farmed fish, and eggs, according to *Poore and Nemecek,* published in *Science* in June 2018.

Animal Cruelty

Something that many people do not know is that animals for human consumption are NOT protected by the laws that protect other animals because they are considered consumer goods, that is, objects. This lends itself to excessive cruelty on behalf of livestock industries. In a 20-minute documentary narrated by the ex-Beatle, Paul McCartney, the reality of the life of farm animals is documented. It can be watched free of cost at meat.org.

What is the difference between vegetarians and vegans?

Vegetarians eat everything but animal meat, including nuts, cereals, root tubers, seaweed, and seeds. Vegetarians do not eat fish, contrary to what many people think (yes, fish are animals ☺). Those are called pescatarians, who eat fish but not any other type of animal.

Vegans do not even consume animal products like cheese, honey, or eggs. An organic vegan diet has the least impact on the production of GHG, equal to driving a car for 281 km in a year. A meat diet even if it were organic, is equivalent to driving a car 4,377 km a year, about 15 times more gas emissions that heat our planet than an organic vegan diet. And it gets worse if not organic; a conventionally meat diet is equivalent to 4,758 km per year, close to 17 times more emissions!

Antibiotics in Meat and Milk

Another factor that causes environmental pollution are the antibiotics used by the livestock industry. These constitute 80% of all antibiotics used in the USA! That is, only 20% of the antibiotic used are to treat people. And on top of this, they are used routinely, not only when animals are sick. This practice

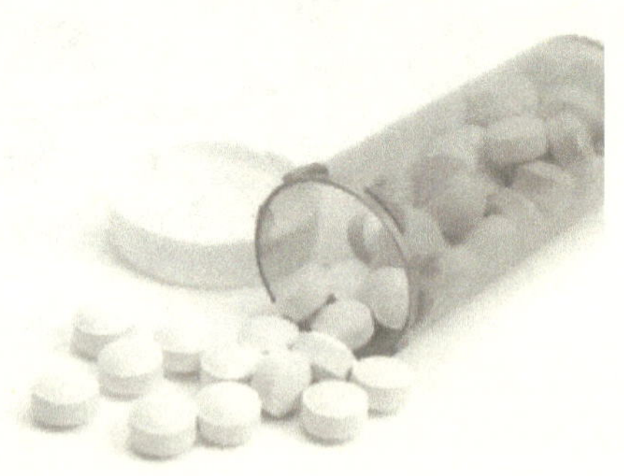

contributes to the development of antibiotic-resistant bacteria. The antibiotics used for animals reach all of us, contaminating soil, bodies of water, and entering our food chain: meat and dairy products.

Meat and Water

Water is one of the resources that will be scarcer due to climate change according to IPCC models. The Stockholm International Water Institute (SIWI) states that by the year 2050, either we all become vegetarians, or we will die for lack of water.[66] A similar statement was stated by the Worldwatch Water Institute.[67].

A plant-based diet can also benefit the economy, according to an article published by the World Economic Forum (WEF) in 2018 [68] and by a study published in the Proceedings of the National Academy of Sciences (PNAS). This research showed that an animal-based diet could cost the US between $197 billion and $289 billion per year[69]. The findings also determined that the global economy stands to lose up to $1.6 trillion by 2050.

---

[66] www.huffpost.com/entry/vegetarian-water-food-shortage_n_1836273
[67] www.worldwatch.org/node/549
[68] www.weforum.org/agenda/2018/12/vegetarianism-is-good-for-the-economy-too/
[69] Springmann et al. (2016), "Analysis and valuation of the health and climate change cobenefits of dietary change", PNAS, retrieved from www.pnas.org/content/pnas/early/2016/03/16/1523119113.full.pdf

Henceforth, it makes sense to begin making modifications now, shifting our patterns of consumption in order to leave a habitable planet for the next generations.

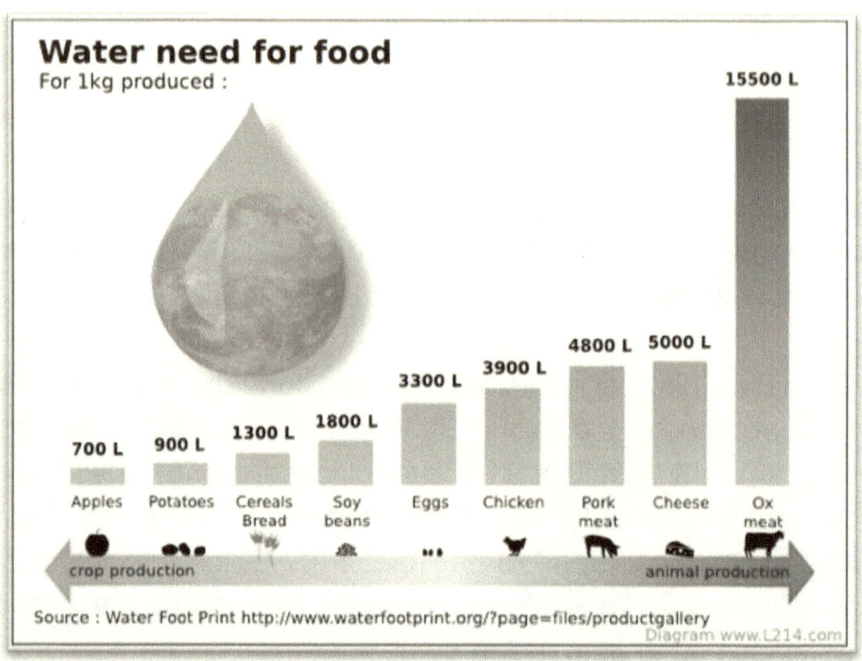

This graph from www.waterfootprint.org and www.L214.com shows the water needed on average to produce 1 pound of each type of food. For example, 700 liters of water are required to produce one pound of apples. To produce one pound of beef, 15,500 liters of water are required, about 22 times more water! So, in addition to taking shorter showers, you can save even more water by changing your diet.

You can learn recipes and vegetarian versions of your typical family or country recipes and also try new recipes from other countries.

Meat and Deforestation

And finally, here we present the amount of land that is used to produce meat. On average, 70% of the land worldwide is used for raising cattle [70] not for growing produce. In addition to that, over 80% of all cereal crops planted and harvested are destined to feed animals, not people. These two factors intensify the deforestation of the planet and the use of petroleum-based agrochemicals that contaminate our soils and water reserves and that have been linked to numerous diseases.

For instance, in the Amazonas, in Brazil, more and more land is devoted to planting cereals mostly destined for use as animal feed. Fires are used to clear the land from trees for transforming it from rainforest into pastures for animal grazing or fields for animal feed. Deforestation also affects the natural hydrological cycle; less trees means no rain events and therefore droughts. Last August a record number of fires propagated for a vast amount of land in Brazil. This was captured by the Atmospheric Infrared Sounder (AIRS) on NASA's Aqua satellite managed by NASA's Jet Propulsion Laboratory in Pasadena, California, as seen on the image below. [71]

---

[70] www.fao.org/docrep/016/ap106e/ap106e.pdf
[71] www.jpl.nasa.gov/spaceimages/details.php?id=PIA23356

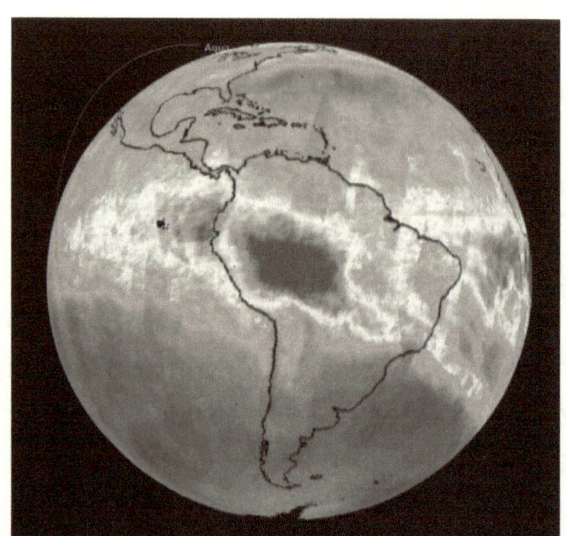

The NASA 's Aqua satellite captured fires from the Amazon region in Brazil from Aug. 8-22, 2019. Red color indicates highest intensity of carbon monoxide. Source: NASA JPL at Caltech.

Some countries, like Ireland, are already starting to encourage changes in the amount of cattle raised in order to reduce its emissions and tackle climate change.[72]

Agrochemicals are used in greater quantity when growing cereals destined for animals feed. That is why we outlined from the beginning of this book, that the current famine problem is not due to global overpopulation as it is sometimes cited: just consider that 100 acres of land can feed 50 meat eaters or 400 to 600 vegans[73], equivalent to 7 to 20 times more people.

---

[72] www.thejournal.ie/farming-climate-change-4770399-Aug2019/

[73] https://michaelbluejay.com/veg/environment.html

Currently the planet produces enough food to feed 10-20 billion people, but a great part goes to waste, and the world's population is only 7 billion. If we were all vegetarians, we could feed many more billions! [74] [75] [76]

So, when people say we need to produce more food to meet the demand, they are really referring to the demand to waste over 50% of food produced! It doesn't make sense, nor does it seem to be an intelligent solution to our global crisis.

9.1.9 Eat Less

Another important factor to consider in order to eat ecologically is to learn to "listen to your stomach", as the Japanese do, thus avoiding eating out of anxiety, pleasure, nervousness, or any other wrong reason.

Many times, what we feel is actually thirst, not hunger. Maintaining a healthy weight for your height decreases your risk of many diseases. Obesity and overweight are linked to increased risk of cancer of the esophagus, breast, endometrium, colon, liver, pancreas, thyroid, heart attack, high blood pressure, diabetes, and other chronic diseases according to the National Cancer Institute.

---

[74] www.fao.org/fileadmin/templates/wsfs/docs/expert_paper/How_to_Feed_the_World_in_2050.pdf

[75] www.theguardian.com/lifeandstyle/2010/jul/18/vegetarianism-save-planet-environment

[76] www.nature.com/articles/s41586-018-0594-0.epdf

Remember that consuming less, also helps the planet since it uses less resources, and decreases your risk to these diseases. Around 75% of the population in the U.S. and 70% of the population in Puerto Rico suffer from overweight, and often times it is not just from overeating, but also because we do not know how to choose healthy, satisfying food.

Eating less is better for the planet due to at least two factors: it reduces food production (deforestation, agrochemicals, transportation, water use, etc.) and reduces the use of drugs due to the improvement in the health of the population.

9.1.10 Choose Healthy Food and Healthy Oils

Finally, here we mention some produce that is very good for you, and some of which can be planted in your backyard (depending on where you live). Some, like turmeric, can even be planted in a pot inside your home, and are very versatile and good for your health.

On the last section of this chapter, we show you which oils are healthy and at what temperature to use them. Remember, your body needs fat. Just don't overdo it.

Turmeric is plant from the ginger family, but it is not spicy and is orange inside. It has anti-inflammatory properties, and many other medicinal properties. It can be used to color your food or for tea.

When planted on the ground, it produces more flowers. In the pictures above, there are two types of turmeric: one with mainly pink flowers and one with flowers purple. They both have some yellow and white petals too. There is also a species with white flowers among many others. The root is easy to grasp and harvest, since it grows almost on top of the soil.

Açai

It is a berry from a palm tree that has been consumed for centuries by the Amazon natives in Brazil. It is very nutritious and grows well in Puerto Rico and other tropical and subtropical climates. It contains many antioxidants, vitamin A, fiber, healthy fats, minerals, vitamin B-12, among others.

Healthy oils

And finally remember that it is important to minimize the use of oils and never to pour used cooking oil down the drain since 1 gallon of oil can contaminate up to 1 million gallons of water [77] , affecting our soil and waterbodies, and marine life.

There are several factors to consider when buying cooking oils, such as the content of **trans fats**, which do not even exist in nature and should always be

---

[77]   https://mnortonville.com/wp-content/uploads/2018/09/above-ground-storage-tank-fact-sheet.pdf

avoided. Unfortunately, that is an ingredient found in most margarines.

On the other hand, there are several types of saturated fats, some are good, while others are harmful to your health. Coconut oil has good, saturated fats and helps raise your good cholesterol level (HDL)[78]. Coconut oil tends to raise good cholesterol, HDL, and lower bad cholesterol, LHL, according to studies published in the Philippine Journal of Cardiology.[79]

Another factor to consider is whether the oil can stand high temperatures, which is defined by its *smoke point*. Many oils are not healthy when used at high temperatures. For example, regular olive oil is good for salads (it has a smoke point of 320°F or 160°C), but not for cooking, unless it is at low or medium heat, or if it is extra virgin olive (EVO) oil, which has a smoking point of 420°F (214°C).

In summary:

Healthy oils for cooking: sunflower, avocado, coconut, butter, Extra Virgin olive (EVO) oil, palm oil (buy only if it is from a sustainable source), almond oil and grapeseed oil.

---

[78] Chinwong et al., "*Daily Consumption of Virgin Coconut Oil Increases High-Density Lipoprotein Cholesterol Levels in Healthy Volunteers: A Randomized Crossover Trial*" Evid Based Complement Alternat Med. 2017; 2017

[79] Dayrit, C. S., "**COCONUT OIL: Atherogenic or Not?** ", Philippine Journal of Cardiology July-September 2003, Volume 31 Number 3:97-104

Salad Oils: olive, hemp, peanut, and flaxseed oils.

In summary, there is no need to go on a diet ... you can eat all that is healthy with moderation: chocolate, desserts, grains, fats, etc., but by eating in moderation and applying these ecological measures we help the planet that we leave to our children, and at the same time, we become healthier.

10   GREEN ECONOMY

There are countless of social and environmental benefits that result from establishing an ecological economy. Do you know the difference between our current economic model and a sustainable economy? Our current economic model is based on the concept of unlimited growth. Nowadays, for most people, it is not enough to have what is necessary to live, most individuals want to get rich, or as the Bruno Mars' song goes– "I *wanna be a billionaire* ♪"

This would only be possible if the planet's resources were unlimited, but that is not the case. The reality is that our planet has limited resources and is more fragile than what we would like to think. Or as the economist *Kenneth Boulding* explains:

> "Anyone who believes that exponential growth can continue forever in a finite world, is a madman or an economist. "- Kenneth Boulding

10.1   Today's Economy

The current economic model encourages the outsourcing of costs. Millions of people pay for these costs with their health and with the pollution of their environment. And as the English economist Arthur

C. Pigou asserted: "Economic actions that impose costs on others should be discouraged."

If we consider that over 300 million people have already been affected by climate disasters according to the IPCC, and of these more than 98% are from developing countries, which are responsible for only 3% of greenhouse gas emissions, we must understand that we have a moral responsibility to take corrective action on this critical issue.

In fact, we are facing several global challenges, global warming, the passage of peak oil production, and the pressure on our ecosystems.

According to James Hansen, former director of NASA Goddard Center, the level of greenhouse gases concentration in our atmosphere must go down to 350 ppm in order to stabilize our climate and maintain a habitable planet.

However, we already reached 410ppm in 2017, and it continues to rise! The latest IPCC report (2018) indicates that we have a little over a decade (until 2030) to avoid irreversible consequences of climate change. To avoid 2.7 F (1.5 C) degrees of warming, according to this report, greenhouse emissions must be reduced by 45% from 2010 levels by 2030.

The good news is that these challenges represent opportunities, to develop and apply green technologies and create green cities and green jobs. The first entities to react to these challenges will have the economic advantage as was the case of Toyota versus GM, which we present later in this chapter. Keep in mind that environmental and economic crises are not separate, but interconnected events, as stated by Stewart Wallis, executive director of the New Economy Foundation or NEF.

According to the 2005 meeting of the United Nations Environment Program (UNEP), more land was converted to agricultural land in the 30 years after 1950 than in the 150 years between 1700 and 1850 [70- 90% is for feeding animals]. The world has lost 50% of its wetlands since 1900 and 35% of the area of mangroves since 1980.

Since 1950, 20% of the original coral reefs surface has been effectively lost and more than 20% are highly degraded or at imminent risk of collapse. The reefs are tremendously important for all human life, providing the equivalent of $375 billion annually in products and services.

The UNEP also ensures that there are four times more water in dams now than in 1960 and 3 to 6 times more water is kept in reserves than in natural rivers. Agriculture accounts for 70% of water use worldwide. The current rate of extinction of species is about 1000 x over what has been throughout the history of the planet.

> **The global forest area has been reduced by 40% during the last 300 years:**
> - **25 countries have completely lost their forests and**
> - **29 countries have less than 10% of their forest cover.**

10.2   Planned obsolescence

…and the externalization of costs

None of these alarming statistics about the state of our ecosystems worldwide are taken into account in the earnings analysis of **conventional economy**. However, they have many social and environmental consequences and a giant economic cost. This is part of what is known as **externalization of costs**.

External costs occur when the production or consumption of a good or service imposes a cost on a third party.

The concept of **Planned Obsolescence**, as we discussed earlier, consists in designing in a way as to limit the useful life of the products, that is, to design them so that they will not last long.

As early as 1932, this concept was presented in the booklet by Bernard London entitled "*End of Depression through Programmed Obsolescence.*" The idea was to encourage people to buy more, without thinking about the consequences.

A classic example of the concept was the light bulb: General Electric and other companies agreed worldwide in the Phoebus cartel[80] of 1921 to limit the life of the bulb to a standard of life of 1,000 hours. Producers were fined if their bulbs lasted longer!

This example is presented in the documentary *The Lightbulb Conspiracy*, which begins with a light bulb that turns 100 years old! This certainly shows that they can be designed to last much longer than 1000 hours. This is equivalent to 4 months, if used 8 hours a day.

10.3   Green Economy

UNEP has developed a definition for green economy given here:

> **A Green Economy produces:**
> **greater social equity, human well-being**
> **and, at the same time, significantly reduces**
> **environmental risks and ecological**

In summary, a green economy is low in emissions, resource-efficient and socially inclusive.

According to NEF, the green economy is necessary and desirable, and it is also possible. The current economic model has failed. The

---

[80] Krajewski, Markus (24 September 2014). "The Great Lightbulb Conspiracy". *IEEE Spectrum http://spectrum.ieee.org/geek-life/history/the-great-lightbulb-conspiracy*

financial crisis exposed deep flaws in the conventional economy approach. Only the minority has benefited from this economy, while the masses are getting poorer.

More than 1/6 of the world's population lives on less than $1 a day. Inequality has risen to unprecedented levels in many developed countries - and the concept of conventional economy... presumes the infinite consumption of finite resources.

It has been scientifically proven that the proliferation of poverty, increases crime rates and violence, and this affects all of us. So that's another good reason to move to a new economic model.

The new economy model is based on giving a real value to things, considering external costs, environmental and social impact. The harmonization among environment, economy, and energy will bring benefits for society in general. A more equitable distribution of goods helps avoid catastrophic and irreversible consequences of climate change.

For this model, the concept of "*Natural Capital*" is defined. The New Definition was developed and published by the U.S. National Academy of Sciences (NAS) in 2016. It consists of a formula to calculate the price of what they call *natural capital* - which includes everything, from groundwater to forests.

This formula will allow politicians and policymakers to compare the value of natural capital with the value of more traditional forms of capital, thus encouraging better investment decisions and more sustainable for the future. Also available online is the InVest tool, which consists of free (open-source software) programs with maps to calculate the value of natural resources.

www.naturalcapitalproject.org/invest/

Likewise, new growth measure metrics have been developed. The traditional ones like the Gross Domestic Product (**GDP**) do not take into account the social or environmental aspects.

The **Genuine Progress Index (GPI)** was developed in the late 1980s by ecological economists Herman Daly and Clifford Cobb. It includes factors such as global warming, pollution, traffic congestion, and depletion of non-renewable resources. It is a more holistic reflection of progress. The term has recently evolved to also include the  cost of crime, given that we now know that poverty increases crime rates.

One of the proposed solutions to reduce greenhouse gas emissions is to create a scheme for the purchase and sale of "carbon credits", known as Cap & Trade. It is a policy for controlling large amounts of emissions from various sources. The approach established for the first time a global cap, which is the maximum amount of emissions per compliance period, for all participating sources. The top is chosen in order to achieve a desired environmental effect.

Some believe that it is not an environmental solution and that it may give large industries the right to contaminate (Hansen, James,

NASA, 2010). Watch the 8-minute video, "The Story of Cap and Trade", available for free on the internet in several languages.

In the following graph we observe an example of the advantages of adopting a sustainable economy. The General Motors (GM) car company in the 90s destroyed the electric car and bought the Hummer. However, the Toyota and Honda produced models of durable and low-emission cars such as hybrids or electric cars. We can see on the graph how sales increased for the companies that offered greener models.

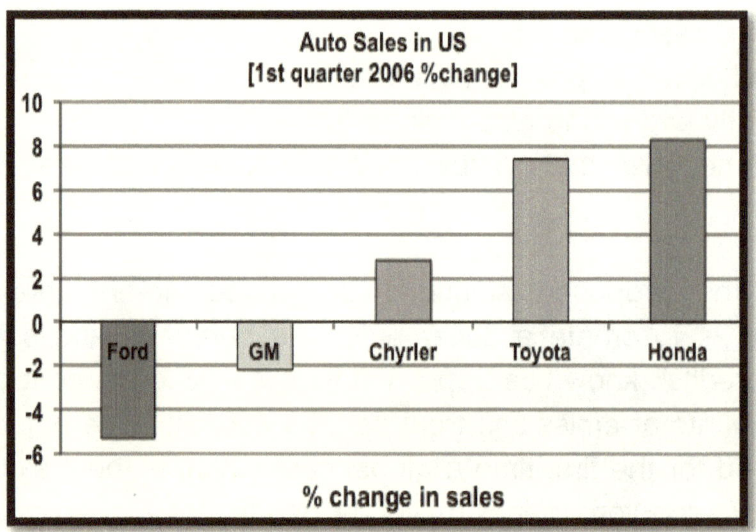

Many times, we hear political leaders say that there is not enough money to implement ecological measures. However, if we look at the long term, the cost of doing nothing will be much greater.

This has been declared again and again by experts in global economics, such as: The DICE model from Yale University, which indicates that "the negative effects of global warming must be assigned a value in ... crucial areas, especially agriculture and the protection of the coasts, and ... (prepare for) possible repercussions."

And as the British economist Sir Nicholas Stern points out, "the potential impacts of climate change on water resources, food production, health, and the environment. ... the global costs of climate change will be equivalent to losing 5% -20% of the world's gross domestic product (GDP) every year, now and forever."!
Professor Weitzman of Harvard, goes further asserting in 2010 that "the risk of a catastrophe, instead of the details of the calculations of cost-benefits, justifies an aggressive climate policy".

Only in Great Britain, the cumulative cost linked to climate change in 2050 can reach up to **$4 trillion**, while that of dealing with social problems linked to inequity would be **$7 trillion**.

The cost of mitigating damages can be many times greater than the investment in green initiatives: impacts on tourism, food (fishing and agriculture), pollution, housing, **social impacts**, health problems, criminality, decadent family social base, ... Stern urges all countries to provide more financial support for research, introduce international product standards and create international programs to explore the best ways to stop deforestation. He also asserts that:

- ■ Climate change must be fully integrated into development policy, and rich countries must fulfill their promises to increase aid through development aid abroad

- ■ International funding to improve regional information on the impacts of climate change

In the meantime, what can we do?

We must abandon the denial and start with the action. Leaving fossil fuels in the ground and switching to renewable energy makes sense, especially in places like Puerto Rice where we do not control prices (especially living in a post- Peak Oil era) and have abundant sun all year round.

We should promote **planning** among all sectors: environment, energy and society, and aggressively apply technology and green policy models applicable to each geography and environment.

The technology exists, now only political will is lacking.

11 REDUCE, RECYCLE, REUSE

Why Reduce is the best option
... and why Recycling is not enough

When we think of ecological measures, many of us think of recycling as something positive, but ... when we analyze the repercussions of recycling and of disposable things, we see the other side of the coin. Is recycling really sustainable? Or are there greener options?

11.1 Why Reduce is the best option

We must begin by recognizing that landfill space is limited. That is especially true in the case of small islands, which have very limited land areas to be designated as civil landfill, and much less for industrial landfills, but it applies to most countries in general.

For instance, in 1994, close to half of the 64 landfills in Puerto Rico had to close due to not being able to comply with the federal regulations of EPA, which involves strict waste management requirements, to minimize the environmental impacts of them and their repercussions on health in general. Later the EPA required the closure of two additional municipal landfills since their operation represented a serious threat to waterbodies and drinking water supplies. Had they not closed; the municipalities were exposed to fines of up to $6,500 per day.

Another part of the problem of garbage management is the lack of education for citizens in general. People throw highly polluting objects to the trash for lack of knowledge about the consequences that these actions have in the quality of the water they drink and other environmental damage that is caused. Examples of these include the inappropriate disposal of household batteries (many of which contain toxic components), cooking oils, paints, fluorescent bulbs, electronic equipment, drugs, and all kinds of materials and objects that are highly polluting the environment in which we live.

In the United States, every day 4.4 pounds of trash are generated per person. In the Puerto Rico, that number is higher, close to 5 pounds! This is more than double the trash a person generates in Europe (1.6 lbs., really 2.8 but 44% is recycled) and is equivalent to 3.65 million tons per year of waste, most of which (90%) ends up in landfills.

Therefore, we must urgently look for ways to drastically reduce the amount of garbage we produce. The incineration of garbage is not the solution because it implies other damages to the environment such as emitting highly toxic gases.

It is necessary to implement urgent measures and actions, such as controlling, reducing, or prohibiting non-recyclable materials such as polystyrene, commonly known as Styrofoam, non-recyclable plastic bottles and containers, single-use plastics, and plastic bags, which are all made from petroleum.

In other countries, actions such as these have contributed to significant reduction of the volume of waste. For example, in China 37 million barrels of oil are saved every year since plastic bags were banned. Australia banned bottled water and some cities in the United States have banned the use of polystyrene. Ireland, Uganda, and some other countries in Europe and Latin America also banned plastic bags and people must bring their own reusable bags every time they go shopping.

This has the added benefit of protecting marine life, including endangered species such as the Leatherback Sea turtle, a species that is greatly affected by thin plastic bags that the wind blow, lift and carry to the ocean, and that these animals confuse with food (jellyfish).

In Puerto Rico plastic bags were banned, but unfortunately, they still sell them in some stores. This is worse since the type of bag they sell is thicker and therefore is harder to decompose. And worse yet, in some stores they dispense paper bags, which foment deforestation.

Another solution to the problem that can reduce the amount of waste that goes to our landfills is to encourage the composting of all organic waste generated at homes, supermarkets, and food and manufacture businesses, transforming them into useful fertilizing material for enrich the soil.

The reduction of waste is definitely critical to solving the problems associated with managing garbage worldwide, and although recycling helps, it does not end this environmental crisis.

> * The priorities, in ecological order, should be:
> 1. Reduce,
> 2. Reuse and
> 3. Recycle

If we reduce, that is, if we buy less things, buy items with less packaging, and reduce consumption in general, then we do not even have to do the other two things: reuse or recycle.

> Recycling is good, but Reducing is much more impactful.

Simple economic and environmental examples of the impact of reducing:

If we buy ready-to-eat gelatin in individual packages, instead of box of powdered gelatin to prepare it, we end up with much more packaging materials that needs to be recycled. Instead of cardboard, you will have to deal with 6-10 plastic containers, and most times that type of plastic is not recyclable in many regions, including Puerto Rico (Since they are not plastic type 1 nor 2).

If we buy bottled water, we pay 1,000 times more than tap water, and we have to think about recycling the bottles. If we drink tap water, which can be filtered, although it is not necessary in many regions, then there is no need to worry about recycling any bottle. If we do not change cell phones so often, we do not have to look for where to recycle them.

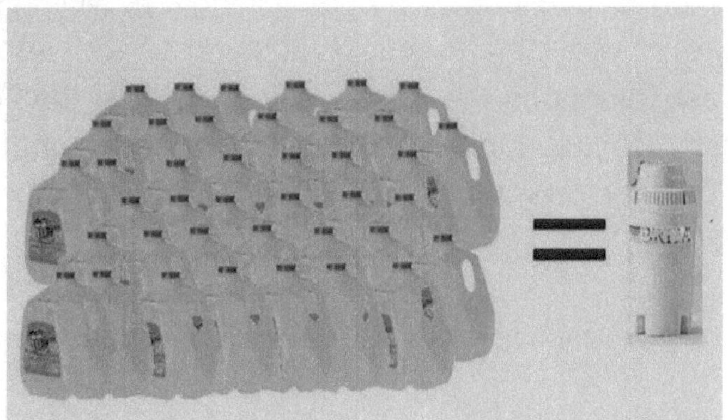

A pitcher filter equals 40 gallons, and saves between $200 to $500 annually, also greatly reduces the volume of waste.

This figure shows that a water jar filter is equivalent to 40 gallons, and thus using a water-filtering jar saves you between $200 to $500 annually, but more importantly, it significantly reduces the volume of waste.

In the case of the cafeteria of the University of Puerto Rico in Mayagüez, changing from disposable (single-use plates, cups and cutlery) to reusable dinnerware could save about $6,000 every month. In the case of batteries, we can save $100 for each rechargeable battery we use and decrease the volume of waste by 99%!

We must all do our share and remember that, if we are not part of the solution, we become part of the problem.

11.2   Recycling Plastic: Common mistakes

One of the biggest challenges in establishing a recycling program is getting people to recycle correctly. It is common for people, usually with the best intentions, to throw away plastics that cannot be recycled into recycling bins, thus contaminating the material to be recycled. The most common mistake is throwing <u>plastic cups and straws</u>.

Why can't most plastics cups, straws, and other containers be recycled?

Although at first glance all plastics look the same, there are many varieties of materials that are all known as plastic. The common feature is that virtually all plastics and styrene are petroleum products. But each one has different properties such as the melting point temperature and how many times it can be recycled before it degrades to a point where it can no longer be used.

For these reasons it is essential to learn to classify them to determine whether it can be recycled or not. First, find the triangular recycling symbol, usually on the bottom of bottles. Look at the number inside the triangle. In most cities recycling companies only accept plastic type # 1 and # 2. (See figure with plastic types). Recycling companies invest a large amount of money in machinery to melt and recycle plastic. Most cannot afford machinery to process plastics with high-melting point like those under categories #3 and up. Other companies simply export the material to countries that use them as raw material to make other products.

Plastics type 1 or 2
Plastic #1 is usually transparent, and is called PET or PETE, meaning "polyethylene terephthalate". Most water and soda bottles are #1. Plastic #2 is called HDPE, which stands for "High-Density Polyethylene" and is opaque. Shampoo, milk, detergents and hygiene product bottles usually fall into category 2 . Both can be recycled easily. Remember to remove the lids as they are usually plastic type 5.

Mixing plastic type # 3 and # 5 like straws and cups with recyclables plastics contaminates the material. **A single type # 3 bottle mixed with 10,000 type # 1 bottles can ruin as it melts, the entire mix destined to be recycled**!

Plastic bags

Even though many plastic bags are classified as plastic type # 2, they should not be included in the recycling with the bottles. This is because they are very difficult to recycle as they become entangled in recycling machines. It is better to separate them and recycle them separately. The best thing for the planet is not to use them at all: use cloth bags for purchases in supermarkets and stores and use biodegradable bags for the trash (which are available in several natural center stores).

If you forget and leave your reusable bags in the car, go back to look for them or carry folding bags in your pocket. Remember that thousands of whales, dolphins, turtles, and other animals die every year, because they confuse plastic bags with jellyfish and ingest them.

On the other hand, plastic # 3 is vinyl, a very toxic material to our health and the environment and one not easy to recycle. Most plastics straws are made of this material and therefore should NOT be thrown into recycling bins.

This type of plastic is characterized by its flexibility. However, multiple studies have linked it with damage to lungs functions, weight gain, insulin resistance, some types of cancer, birth defects, chronic bronchitis, ulcers, vision failures, and low sperm count thus affecting fertility. Remember, plastic straws cannot be recycled. Think whether you really need a straw. You can buy a reusable straw made out of stainless steel or silicone. Lately, many cities are banning plastic straws and people are becoming aware of how detrimental they are for animals, humans and the planet.

This cup and straw contaminate the material to be recycled.

Plastics type 4,5,6

In most countries, only plastics #1 and #2 are recycled. The rest usually needs higher temperatures to recycle and is not as cost effective. So, the #3-#7 recycle symbols (triangles) do not necessarily mean they are recyclable. Check with your local recycling company.

Plastic cups and containers of margarine, and yogurt, are usually plastic type 4, 5 or 6 and therefore cannot be recycled (check with your recycling company to see if their specifications change). In addition, many of them have been related to diseases including cancer. See details in the table on this link https://ecologycenter.org/factsheets/adverse-health-effects-of-plastics/.

Try to buy products that come in glass containers; they are healthier, and you can reuse them to store homemade jellies or other recipes.

Look for alternatives such as biodegradable cups made from vegetable waste such as corn, potatoes, or bamboo. But the most environmentally friendly by far are reusable objects, such as metal or ceramic cups. It is always cheaper to use dishes that can be washed and reused over and over again.

Plastics within Category # 7 refer to all other plastic materials that do not fall into the first 6 categories, including polystyrene or foam (Styrofoam®). The latter is highly toxic, having been associated with respiratory, gastro-intestinal, and nervous system diseases (fatigue, nervousness, and difficulty sleeping), and with low hemoglobin count, among others. Furthermore, scientific studies show that styrene molecules cause cancer in laboratory animals.

The problem is that cups and plates made of polystyrene infiltrate styrene to the food, which are then ingested by people. The hotter the food that is served on them, the more it infiltrates these chemicals into the foods, and the same effect happens if they are used in the microwave oven; they release more toxins into the food.

Another serious problem with polystyrene is it never biodegrades, remaining eternally in nature; it continues to fragment into microscopic pieces that are ingested by small animals and thus infiltrate our food chain. It is also a very difficult material to recycle.

Thousands of birds are victims of our trash, which they confuse with food. Source: www.nextnature.net/2009/10/plastic-birds/

Perhaps in part because of the use of so much plastic today there are three times more cancer today than 100 years ago. Cancer today is more common, even in young children, who are more susceptible to the effect of these chemicals because their organs are in development.

Recycle Properly

In short, improper recycling can bring bad consequences, including the fact that the company might decide to stop coming to collect the material to be recycled in order to minimize its losses.

Recycling correctly saves a lot of energy and resources and decreases the volume of garbage in landfills, decreasing the methane they produce and their effect on global warming. Other important facts:

- The vast majority of plastic bottles are produced with resin that comes from petroleum.

- Most bottles are not recycled into a new bottle, but reused to make other products such as bags, carpets, and blankets. In other words, recycling bottles does not prevent the production of more bottles using virgin petroleum.

- A plastic bottle takes more than 500 years to appear invisible. It stays in nature forever. Plastic waste is not biodegradable, so, if it is not recovered or recycled, it causes great damage to the earth, and to the fauna. And we are part of the fauna.

- Most bottled water is tap water! It is better to buy a water filter and fill a reusable stainless-steel bottle with filtered water. You will save a lot of money and you will be helping your health and the Planet!

Advantages of Recycling:

- Reduces the volume and the need for landfills and incineration.

- Conserves natural resources.

- Saves energy and prevents pollution caused by the extraction and processing of virgin materials and the manufacture of products using natural resources.

- It reduces the emissions of greenhouse gases that contribute to global warming.

- It helps sustain the environment for future generations.

- Recovering two tons of plastic is equivalent to saving a ton of petroleum oil.

Better than Recycling

However, we must always remember that much more important and beneficial than recycling is to reduce. In fact, that is the most important of all the R's.

We only have one planet, and it is already giving serious signals in all parts of the globe of a climatological imbalance, due to our daily living practices. It is up to all of us as good global citizens to take care of the planet that we leave to future generations, and this requires changes in our habits. It is time to reevaluate and modify our behavior, to educate ourselves on how to live sustainably. In the long run, we all benefit.

12 Consequences Of What We Buy

Did you know that every decision you make about what to buy has an impact on the lives of other human beings who are worth as much as you?

In this chapter you will learn about the environmental, social, and economic impact of what we buy and how to choose products that minimize these impacts.

I invite you to look for three pieces of clothing or other objects that you own and locate on the label their place of origin.

Everything we buy has environmental, social and economic consequences. Maybe if we knew them, we would think twice before buying and consume less. We have become a consumer society. Marketing campaigns make us believe that to be happy we need to buy more and more. The reality is that after satisfying basic needs such as food, clothing, and shelter, having more does not increase happiness, but, on the contrary, brings complexity and concerns into our lives.

As the humorist Art Buchwald says, "the best things in life are not things". Note also that it is a challenge to get things that are not manufactured in places where there is child labor.

There are many countries where slavery still exists and there are no safety regulations for working conditions.

Our insatiable appetite for what shines and for appearances, make us keep high demand for precious metals such as gold, but working conditions in gold mines are extremely deplorable. Do you remember from Chapter 6, the mercury that is produced in these mines? It is highly toxic. If the gold was used only for electronic equipment, the mines could be closed, and we would probably be able to give these young people a more dignified and healthy job.

If we buy fish from Thailand we are indirectly and unknowingly promoting labor slavery. Thousands of young people are kidnapped annually with deceitful promises of decent work to help their families and then they are tied with chains to boats where they have to spend the rest of their lives fishing and living with a poor diet and without communication with their relatives. Many do not survive.

You might remember the case of a fisherman from Burma who managed to escape after 22 years of slavery in July 2015.

That's why the prices of these fish are low, and we can consume it in large quantities. In developed countries the "All-you-can-eat buffets" abound, where people served large quantities of food and where a ridiculously high percentage of that food is wasted. In fact, in the United States almost fifty percent (50%) of the food goes to waste, for several reasons.

The documentary "Walmart: the High Cost of Low Price" presents the working conditions of thousands of employees who have had to leave their families in rural areas to come to the city to work six days a week between 10 to 14 hours a day with such low pay that it makes it impossible for them to get out of this lifestyle and exposed to toxins that can even affect their reproductive organs and cause many diseases.

In this documentary, one of the employees interviewed, begs the viewers not to buy products made in China. Why? Remember that many of these products come with toxics, some banned in the United States and other countries; but toys or shoes never come with a list of ingredients, so there is no way to know. Most don't last long and poison our health and the environment reminding us of the old saying "Cheap is expensive." We pay with our health, the environment, and the living conditions of other beings.

Do you remember the collapse of the sewing factory building in Bangladesh in 2013? More than a thousand people lost their lives, and over two thousand were injured. The structure of the building was plagued by structural failures, terrible electrical connections, lack of air circulation, and other unsafe conditions.

They were making clothes for an extremely low cost for companies that then sell these clothes at unreachable prices for them and even sometimes expensive for us.

Another documentary, "**The Dark Side of Chocolate**", presents the sad reality of millions of children on the African continent. They are deceived with promises of work or are kidnapped when they go for a walk and taken to other countries where they do not even speak the language. They have to spend the rest of their lives working on cocoa farms, without ever even knowing what the huge cocoa pods they grow are for. This is the case for seventy-five percent (75%) of the chocolate in the world, including the most popular brands. The movie is free to watch at www.slavefreechocolate.org.

The documentary "**The Dark Side of Chocolate**", presents the sad reality of millions of children forced to work like slave on cocoa plantations.

For example, Nestlé, Hershey, and Mars are being sued for helping and instigating human rights violations by buying cocoa from the Ivory Coast. The Ferrero company recently indicated that it hopes to eradicate slavery from the farms where it gets its cocoa by the year 2020.

Chocolate is also harvested in Puerto Rico and Latin America, which is where most of the organic chocolate comes from. Organic farms are monitored frequently, perhaps for this reason they do not usually have slave children. In this link you can see a list of companies that produce cocoa ethically www.slavefreechocolate.org.

What can we do to avoid or reduce this kind of social impact of what we buy? You can make ensure that you are not promoting practices of human trafficking and slavery by buying products with the Fair-trade seal. It also helps if you buy previously used articles at Vintage, Thrift, or Goodwill stores (usually managed by the US Salvation Army), and finally, buying less and buying quality products with classic and durable styles.

Every time you go shopping,
  ask yourself these questions:

- Do I need it?
- Can I buy it used?
- What are the impacts to the environment and society?

Remember, buying local helps the country's economy, minimizes emissions due to transportation, and ensures that you do not sponsor slave labor.

The 1.5-minute video titled "The 2 Euro T-Shirt - A Social Experiment" analyzes what would happen if people really knew what lies behind what we buy. It shows the power of education. When we buy low quality, things last a short time, which again reminds us of the saying "cheap is expensive". In addition, they often contain toxic products that slowly make us sick. Buying quality is worth it. In the long run you save a lot of money and the impact of buying cheap products of poor quality lasts a long time in the landfill, sometimes forever, depending on the material.

Learning to live in harmony with nature will bring us peace-of-mind, better economy, health, and the great satisfaction of knowing that we are doing the right thing, that our ecological footprint is less, and it helps the lives of other beings in distant places on the planet that are worth as much as we.

In this book I have shown you many ways to save money with ecological measures. In my case, applying these measures have saved my thousands of dollars per year. The following table summarizes my typical yearly savings.

Green $aving$

Description	Yearly Savings
Electricity bill	$1000-$4000
Water bill	$50-$130
Drinking water	$200-$1000
gasoline	$300-$1000
Paper Towels	$30
Beauty products	$50-400
Not smoking	$3000
Dry cleaning	$10-100
Disposable dinnerware	$20-100
Food habits - Ecotarian	$750 per person
Medicines for asthma, Medical expenses	$?
Cook at home, reducing packaging	$?
TOTAL	Your call!

How can you use your ecological savings, which can add up to thousands of dollars annually?

Buy organic products, you will save on medicine later. It is like investing in your future and in your retirement. And above all, disseminate what you have learned among your family and friends, it will make a big difference for them too. So, every day we will be building a better planet for future generations.

13 CLIMATE DISEASE

The spread of diseases is also augmented by changes in temperatures and the climate.

Did you know that some pests are confined to certain geographical regions due to the environmental temperature? For example, many mosquitoes and rodents do not reach certain regions because they are very cold or very arid. With climate change, many pests like these are spreading to places where they were never seen before, carrying with them diseases to these areas.

Several studies, such as one from the Wildlife Conservation Society, have identified diseases that have worsened due to climate change[81]. Among them:

1. Aviary Flu (H5N1)
2. Babesiosis
3. Cholera
4. Ebola
5. Lyme disease
6. The plague
7. Red algae blooms
8. Tuberculosis
9. Yellow fever
10. Malaria
11. Dengue

Mail Online
Home | News | U.S. | | Money
Outbreak of rare rat virus linked to acute kidney disease sparks panic in the Midwest
· Eight people have been diagnosed with the Seoul virus in Wisconsin and Illinois
· The outbreak has come from rat farms in the states, officials confirmed
· Officials are investigating how the foreign virus reached the United States
· It can cause fever, chills, nausea, aches, irritated skin, and hemorrhages
By DAILYMAIL.COM REPORTER and ASSOCIATED PRESS
PUBLISHED: 23:54 BST, 20 January 2017 | UPDATED: 23:54 BST, 20 January 2017

---

[81] Scientific American, "Deadly by the Dozen: 12 Diseases Climate Change May Worsen". Oct. 2008

According to the United Nations, some of these diseases affect not only humans but also animals. Across the globe, there have been increases in diseases such as HIV/AIDS, hantavirus, hepatitis C, SARS, and others.

In 2017, huge amounts of flowers appeared in deserts in the USA and were even visible from space. This might look beautiful, but unfortunately it encouraged the reproduction of rats and mice that carry the *hanta* virus, which produces internal hemorrhages.

As temperatures continue to rise, we will have to deal with more diseases and unthinkable challenges, and this also represents economic expenses for society. The faster we react, the better our chances to minimize climate change impacts on all species, including us. According to the latest report from the IPCC, we have about a decade (until 2030) to lower the concentration of GHG to avoid the point of no return, which would mean chaotic extreme weather and enormous loss of life and resources.

We still have time to save us from this climate crisis, but we need to act fast. By reading this book, you already took the first step, which is education. Keep learning and changing your habits to reduce your impact on the planet. And more importantly, demand your leaders to take action and implement environmental measures in your country.

This way, everybody wins.

14 ADDITIONAL REFERENCES

Where can you find more information? Remember not to believe everything that appears published either on the internet or social networks or even on paper. Check the authors' affiliations and source of funding of research to see how reliable they are. Peer-reviewed journals are more reliable, while some magazines are not refereed and practically anyone can publish.

- American Cancer Society www.cancer.org/
- American Institute for Cancer Research www.aicr.org/
- BBC, March 19, 2008, *"Vegan Diet 'help' for arthritis"*, http://news.bbc.co.uk/2/hi/health/7301188.stm
- Callewaert, C. E.De Maeseneire, F. Kerckhof, A. Verliefde, T. Van de Wiele and N. Boon, (2014), *"Microbial Odor Profile of Polyester and Cotton Clothes after a Fitness Session"*, Appl Env. Microbiol. www.ncbi.nlm.nih.gov/pmc/articles/PMC4249026/
- Cambio Climático Global, Retrieved February 06, 2017 http://cambioclimaticoglobal.com
- Cancer Research UK, http://info.cancerresearchuk.org/
- Climate Central, (2019), Hottest Years on Record Globally,www.climatecentral.org/gallery/graphics/the-10-hottest-global-years-on-record
- Cole, S. , (Feb 2015), NASA Headquarters, "2014 warmest year in modern record", http://climate.nasa.gov/news/2221/
- *Dr. R. A. Oppenlander explains why even Free-Range Organic Meat harms the Planet and your Health* http://comfortablyunaware.com/
- EPA, Metal Index, www.epa.gov/methane/index.html

- EPA, Pesticides, (Retrieved 2019) www.epa.gov/pesticides/health/cancerfs.htm
- Epstein, P. R., & Ferber, D. (2011, April 01). Malaria on the Rise as East African Climate Heats Up. Retrieved from www.scientificamerican.com/article/east-africa-malaria-rises-under-climate-change/
- Eshel G. and P.A., Martin, (2005) *Diet, Energy, and Global Warming, Earth Interactions.*
- FAO (Food and Agriculture Organization of the United Nations), Mandates and Reports, Retrieved 2019 from http://www.fao.org/organicag/oa-mandate/en/
- FAO Commission / OMS Codex Alimentarius, 1999, Retrieved from
- FAO Promotes Organic Agriculture, http://www.i-sis.org.uk/FAOPromotesOrganicAgriculture.php
- FAO, Sustainable Agriculture, (2019), www.fao.org/sustainability/en/
- Gallagher, J., BBC News, (April 2013*), "Red meat chemical 'damages heart', say US scientists", http://www.bbc.com/news/health-22042995*
- Gichigi, A. (2016, January 23). Climate change and malaria in Nairobi. Retrieved February 04, 2017, from www.irinnews.org/feature/2007/07/31
- Green Alliance, (Jan 2015), **A Circular Economy for Smart Devices** www.green-alliance.org.uk/resources/A%20circular%20economy%20for%20smart%20devices.pdf
- Guardian, The, "We're all losers to a gadget industry built on planned obsolescence". (2015, March 23). www.theguardian.com/sustainable-business/2015/mar/23/were-are-all-losers-to-gadget-industry-built-on-planned-obsolescence
- Healthy cooking oils https://jonbarron.org/diet-and-nutrition/healthiest-cooking-oil-chart-smoke-points
- http://goveg.com/environment-globalwarming.asp
- http://www.bbc.co.uk/news/health-22042995
- http://www.un.org/apps/news/story.asp?NewsID=20772&Cr=global&Cr1=environment
- https://blogs.scientificamerican.com/news-blog/spam-junk-email-wastes-energy-2009-04-16/

- HuffingtonPost, *"Scientists Predict The World's Population Will Become Vegetarian By 2050"*, (2012), www.huffingtonpost.ca/2012/08/27/vegetarian-diet-scientist_n_1834182.html
- Justin Worland, *"How Climate Change Could Spread Diseases Like Zika"*, Time Magazine, Jan 2016
- Keele Universitty Birchall Centre, bioinorganic Chemistry of Aluminium and Silicon www.keele.ac.uk/aluminium/mediaandpresentations/
- King D., Murray J. (2012). "Climate policy: Oil's tipping point has passed". https://www.nature.com/articles/481433a *Nature.* **481**
- Lista de plantas fijadoras de nitrógeno: www.sergicaballero.com/plantas-fijadoras-de-nitrogeno/
- McMichael, D.H. Campbell-Lendrum, C.F. Corvalán, K.L. Ebi, A. Githeko, J.D. Scheraga and A. Woodward, (2003), WHO: World Health Organization of the United Nations, **Climate Change and Human Health**, Ch. 6, *Climate and Infectious Diseases*, 2003, www.who.int/globalchange/publications/cchhbook/en
- Mercola, (2014), **"Synthetic Fabrics Host More Stench-Producing Bacteria"**, http://articles.mercola.com/sites/articles/archive/2014/09/20/synthetic-polyester-fabrics.aspx
- Minnesota Pollution Control Agency, (2015), "BPA in thermal paper", https://www.pca.state.mn.us/green-chemistry/bpa-thermal-paper#strategies-66f00276
- Mlot, S. (2015, March 13). Good Luck Trying to Fix New MacBook Air, Pro. Retrieved February 06, 2017, Retrieved February, 2017 http://uk.pcmag.com/mac-laptops-products/40411/news/good-luck-trying-to-fix-new-macbook-air-pro
- Mosquito-borne Diseases on the Uptick—Thanks to Global Warming, Scientific American, retrieved May 2017 www.scientificamerican.com/article/mosquito-borne-diseases-on-the-uptick-thanks-to-global-warming/
- National Cancer Institute, (2019), "Artificial Sweeteners and Cancer" www.cancer.gov/cancertopics/factsheet/Risk/artificial-sweeteners

- National Geographic, *¿Qué es Calentamiento Global?*, www.nationalgeographic.es/medio-ambiente/calentamiento-global/calentamiento-global-definicion
- Natural Fiber Clothing http://empoweredsustenance.com/natural-fiber-clothing/
- Organic Agricultura- FAO: www.fao.org/organicag/oa-faq/oa-faq1/en/
- Pesticides and Cancer www.ncbi.nlm.nih.gov/pubmed/9498903
- Reporte de el Panel Inter-gubernamental de Cambio Climático de las Naciones Unidas (UN-IPCC por sus siglas en inglés), (2007, 2014, 2016), www.ipcc.ch
- Ricjström, J, et al., (2009), *"Planetary Boundaries: Exploring the Safe Operating Space for Humanity*, http://pdxscholar.library.pdx.edu/cgi/viewcontent.cgi?article=1063&context=iss_pub
- Rockström, J. et al., (2009), "Planetary Boundaries: Exploring the Safe Operating Space for Humanity", Portland State University https://pdxscholar.library.pdx.edu/cgi/viewcontent.cgi?referer=&httpsredir=1&article=1063&context=iss_pub
- Sandonato,S. and H. Willebald, (2018), *"Natural Capital, Domestic Product and Proximate Causes of Economic Growth: Uruguay in the Long Run*", Special Issue Natural Resources Economics. https://www.mdpi.com/2071-1050/10/3/715
- Schmidt, L. J. (2017, January 31). Satellite data confirm annual carbon dioxide minimum above 400 ppm. http://climate.nasa.gov/news/2535/satellite-data-confirm-annual-carbon-dioxide-minimum-above-400-ppm/
- Sustainable Agricultura: www.sustainabletable.org/246/sustainable-agriculture-the-basics
- The Cancer Project www.cancerproject.org/
- The Guardian, "Caribbean coral reefs 'will be lost within 20 years' without protection", Retrieved February 06, 2017 www.theguardian.com/environment/2014/jul/02/caribbean-coral-reef-lost-fishing-pollution-report
- Thompson, A., (2007), *"Global Warming Might Spur Earthquakes and Volcanoes",* LiveScience, Retrieved from www.livescience.com/7366-global-warming-spur-earthquakes-volcanoes.html

- Tomljenovic L, 2011, *"Aluminum and Alzheimer's disease: after a century of controversy, is there a plausible link?"*, Journal of Alzheimer D. www.ncbi.nlm.nih.gov/pubmed/21157018
- UN World Health Organization www.who.int/
- University of Chicago, EurekAlert! AAAS,, (Apr 2006), *"Study: Vegan diets healthier for planet, people than meat diets"*,www.eurekalert.org/pub_releases/2006-04/uoc-svd041306.php
- Vyawahare, M, (2015), *"Hawaii First to Harness Deep-Ocean Temperatures for Power"* ClimateWire, www.scientificamerican.com/article/hawaii-first-to-harness-deep-ocean-temperatures-for-power/
- World Cancer Research Fund - www.wcrf-uk.org/
www.fao.org/organicag/oa-faq/oa-faq1/en/

About the Author ...

For over 25 years, Sandra Cruz-Pol was a professor in the Department of Electrical and Computer Engineering at the University of Puerto Rico in Mayagüez (UPRM). She earned her Ph.D. in Electrical Engineering from Penn State University working with satellite sensors studying atmospheric greenhouse gases and ocean emissivity. She worked with radars to study properties of the oceans and the atmosphere at the University of Massachusetts, and later with radars studying cloud microphysics. She has worked on several projects sponsored by NASA and NSF, including a Doppler meteorological radar network deployed on the island of Puerto Rico. She also served as the Program Director of the National Science Foundation (NSF) in the Electromagnetic Radiofrequency Spectrum Division and is currently a Program Director for the Engineering Research Center program.

In addition, Dr. Cruz-Pol was a member of the Radio Frequency Committee (CORF) of the National Academy of Sciences (NAS) of the United States, and a member of the technical committee for the IEEE Frequencies Allocations in Remote Sensing (FARS). Dr. Cruz-Pol received the NASA Faculty Award for Research in 2001.

Dr. Cruz-Pol identified the need to establish a structure organized in UPRM to address the problems and find solutions to tackle climate change and founded the Green Campus initiative in UPRM in 2007. She has developed a large amount of informative and educational materials, presentations, activities, initiatives, and websites on sustainability issues. He has a blog called Ahorro$ Verde$ (Green Saving$) in the newspaper El Nuevo Día available online. She has offered hundreds of talks to different types of audience, from elementary level K-12 to the general public and at university and professional level. Green Campus is affiliated with the Roots and Shoots chapters of Dr. Jane Goodall.